REFLECTIVE PRACTICE AND PROFESSIONAL DEVELOPMENT

Burs

Education at SAGE

SAGE is a leading international publisher of journals, books, and electronic media for academic, educational, and professional markets.

Our education publishing includes:

- accessible and comprehensive texts for aspiring education professionals and practitioners looking to further their careers through continuing professional development
- inspirational advice and guidance for the classroom
- authoritative state of the art reference from the leading authors in the field

Find out more at: **www.sagepub.co.uk/education**

REFLECTIVE PRACTICE AND PROFESSIONAL DEVELOPMENT

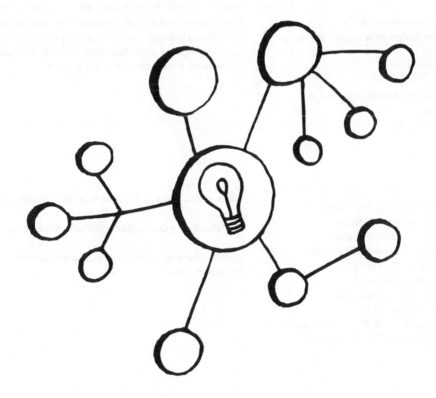

PETER TARRANT

Los Angeles | London | New Delhi
Singapore | Washington DC

Los Angeles | London | New Delhi
Singapore | Washington DC

SAGE Publications Ltd
1 Oliver's Yard
55 City Road
London EC1Y 1SP

SAGE Publications Inc.
2455 Teller Road
Thousand Oaks, California 91320

SAGE Publications India Pvt Ltd
B 1/I 1 Mohan Cooperative Industrial Area
Mathura Road
New Delhi 110 044

SAGE Publications Asia-Pacific Pte Ltd
3 Church Street
#10-04 Samsung Hub
Singapore 049483

© Peter Tarrant, 2013

First published 2013

Commissioning editor: Jude Bowen
Editorial assistant: Miriam Davey
Project manager: Jeanette Graham
Assistant production editor: Thea Watson
Copyeditor: Sharon Cawood
Proofreader: Isabel Kirkwood
Marketing manager: Lorna Patkai
Cover design: Wendy Scott
Typeset by: C&M Digitals (P) Ltd, Chennai, India
Printed and bound by CPI Group (UK) Ltd,
Croydon, CR0 4YY

Library of Congress Control Number: 2012937036

British Library Cataloguing in Publication data

A catalogue record for this book is available from the British Library

MIX
Paper from
responsible sources
FSC
www.fsc.org FSC® C013604

ISBN 978-1-4462-4950-5
ISBN 978-1-4462-4951-2 (pbk)

To Barbara Frame for inspiring me academically
and for believing in me.

To my wife Caroline and my family, for giving
me the space to reflect and write.

To Fergus, Steven, Becky, Rachael and Daniel.

Contents

Acknowledgements

Many colleagues, teachers, students and pupils have helped to make this book possible. Through their support and reflections, it has been possible to develop and test many of the ideas contained herein.

In particular, I would like to thank the following:

BEd Year 4 primary student, September 2008

BEd primary students in their 3rd or 4th year in 2010

PGDE students from 2010, 2011 and 2012

Susan Whatmore and Kelly Watt, PGDE students, 2012

Heather Lucas, PGDE student, 2010

Darren Swan, Roslin Primary School class teacher

Teresa Reid, Roslin Primary School class teacher

Jennifer Allison and the staff and pupils of Roslin Primary School

Deborah Holt, teaching fellow, Moray House School of Education

Morag Crolla, teaching fellow, Moray House School of Education

Melanie Ross, Sciennes Primary School and Primary 7, 2010

About the author

Peter Tarrant is a Teaching Fellow at the University of Edinburgh, where he has worked for the last five years.

He is responsible for the organization and running of a number of courses for Initial Teacher Education. He lectures in Practicum, Professional Studies, Learning Behaviour and Languages and Literacy. He is also responsible for developing Professional Reflection for students on the Bachelor of Education and the Post Graduate Diploma in Education courses.

He previously worked as a primary school head teacher for five years and as a deputy head teacher for 15 years.

The structure and intent of the book

This book aims to encourage the reader to reflect on their professional practice.

It takes a brief look (in Chapters 1, 2 and 3) at what is meant by professionalism and reflection. This is the section where the theoretical underpinning can be found with reference to other significant work in this field.

The next stage (Chapters 3, 4 and 5) is to suggest a different way of encouraging reflection. This is an approach where professionals are encouraged to have greater 'ownership' of their reflections and where they are supported in articulating what those reflections are. In these chapters, we argue that peer learning interactions can be beneficial in terms of professional reflection because they bring the following opportunities:

Benefits of an approach involving peer learning interactions

- Provides personal ownership

- Is non-judgemental

- Develops reflective skills

- Develops articulating skills

- Shows that facilitating is a learning experience in itself

- Describes the experience which makes the reflection more potent

- Gets away from controlling agendas

- Gets over the one-off snapshot approach

- Involves the idea that frequent and focused is better than a nerve-racking one-off observation and feedback

- Has a focus on the future not the past

- Is an enjoyable and collaborative approach to developing practice

In Chapter 6, we look at what students and teachers think of reflective practice and articulated learning interactions. There is evidence here from working with students and teachers over a three-year period.

In Chapter 7, there is information about modifying the approach from reflective practice for adults to 'meta learning' for children. There is a discussion about the potential of the approach and some information about how it has been received in local primary schools.

Chapter 8 looks at supporting reflective practice in practice.

Chapter 9 draws some conclusions about reflective practice and the suggestions contained in this book.

In the Appendices, you will find some useful resources and ideas.

Introduction: Peer Learning and Personal, Professional, Reflective Practice

Although this book attempts to establish the importance of professionalism in general, and reflective professionalism in particular, it is important to have a realistic understanding of the complexity of being a professional. In many professions, the stakes are high, time and money are in short supply, and any suggestion of adding to the burden of daily practice will not receive a positive response. Browsing this book on the bookshelves may lead you to ask the following question:

> On top of everything else that constitutes my professional life, why would I undertake all this reflective practice stuff as well?

Indeed, it is a question that concerns me greatly. In this book, I try to argue the case for an interpretation of professionalism that benefits from, and is supported by, reflective practice. I try to argue that the 'best learning' (the most potent, memorable and lasting) is that which we learn for ourselves. Yet ultimately, it is the commitment and professionalism of the individual that will make it a success. Ideally, the individual will want to engage in reflective practice, they will want to look at their practice on a regular basis, and to use what they learn to continue to develop in their profession.

However, this kind of professional, who is motivated and self-aware enough to undertake this path, will be very rare. The best chance of success is for there to be an institutional focus or commitment to reflection. If the company, authority, service, school or institution commit to this approach, and if they encourage, organize and support staff then there is much more chance of success. Without this support and commitment, it is all too easy to put such matters aside, claiming that the job is already much too difficult, time too short and priorities elsewhere much more demanding.

As Wenger (2006) explains: 'A growing number of associations, professional and otherwise, are seeking ways to focus on learning through reflection on practice. Their members are restless and their allegiance is fragile.'

The ideas in this book, and the view of authentic, professional, reflective practice as something self-initiated and self-perpetuating are an ideal. This ideal, it must be acknowledged, needs the support of the institution in order to succeed.

I have seen this approach introduced in schools where staff were initially very keen and enthusiastic about the idea, but where early impetus floundered due to a lack of institutional support. Once introduced, little was said or done to support and encourage staff to be involved. In this situation, even the most committed professional will lose heart and devote their attention to more pressing matters.

Yet in other contexts, I have seen management, who were committed to the success of the approach, support and facilitate in a way that enabled time and space to be found; where the dialogue and topic of reflection were constantly kept high on the agenda. In these situations, the staff flourished, as did the school ethos and reflective conversation.

Staff may be self-motivated enough to volunteer and organize reflective sessions for themselves. They may get involved because they are persuaded and encouraged by others; they may be coerced by their management; but the best scenario will be where the institution takes professionalism seriously and makes a commitment to develop reflective practice as a priority. If there is full backing, with some kind of training for those involved and time devoted to setting up the scheme, there will be more chance of success. Thereafter, it will be important to check that sessions are happening on a regular basis until the ethos is well embedded into the institution.

As a researcher investigating the effectiveness of the approach, it would be easy to decide that it was a big success because, every time you visit the staff, they are all involved and speak highly of the benefits of the approach. However, it is what happens afterwards that is the acid test. Will staff still be involved when there isn't the prospective visit from the researcher looming?

Certainly in ITE we have made this approach an integral part of the placement programme. The peer learning constitutes both formative assessment and student support. It is something that students *must do* in order to progress. The hope and belief is that having spent some time engaged in the scheme, students will then go out into schools and spread the word. One of the aims of this book is to make the whole background to reflective practice and the strategies used clear and accessible so that any institution can set up to involve their workforce. However, as stated above, it is not simply a case of 'here it is, now get on with it'.

If staff feel accountable, in the sense that someone will ask them if they have been involved, or they show an interest in the experience or outcome, there will be more success than if, once introduced, the assumption is that staff will continue unsupported and without encouragement from management.

There is an irony here, of course. Professional reflective articulations rely on the notion that the power imbalance is removed. It thrives on the notion that the professional wants to work things out for themselves, yet there still needs to be some lead, direction or organizational support from management in order to 'make it happen, and enable it to keep on happening'.

The difference lies perhaps in the fact that support, encouragement and interest shown by management are different from the traditional accountability agendas of the past. The involvement that is advocated is more to do with *leadership* and with a management team that has a commitment to an interpretation of staff development which is about 'helping people to help themselves'.

In terms of power relationships, this leadership is all about setting up and supporting an approach which empowers others to develop professionally. Instead of a top-down approach, staff can be part of a professional development dialogue, but they need management to show an interest and encourage them to take part and to continue to do so.

The aim of this book is to highlight the importance and significance of professional reflection, to explore the many ways of encouraging reflection, and to suggest a raft of measures to ensure that reflection becomes an instinctive aspect of any professional's practice. Whilst aimed primarily at students in ITE and teachers in the early stages of their career, it is hoped that other professionals might learn from the discussions regarding reflective practice and ways of achieving an ethos of reflection to support professional development in any institution.

Reference

Wenger, E. (2006) *Communities of Practice: A Brief Introduction*. Available at: www. ewenger.com/theory/

1

What is reflective practice?

Chapter Overview

In this chapter, I will discuss professionalism and the reasons why we are encouraged to reflect. I will look at some of the more traditional models of supporting reflective practice and explore the strengths and weaknesses of these approaches and their impact on practice.

- Why this book?
- Why do we need to reflect?
- What is reflection?
- What is the impact on practice?
- Focus reflection questions

Why this Book?

For many years now, I have been working with teachers and student teachers in developing professionalism. One important element of this professionalism is reflection on practice. Over this time, I have investigated a number of approaches to reflection; and I have investigated the ways it is promoted, 'prescribed,' supported, documented and utilized in the context of teacher professionalism. I have looked at coaching models, structured models and traditional models. I have considered the benefits and drawbacks to reflection and the many challenges in having an approach that encourages personal reflection which is relevant, meaningful, and, above all, useful to those doing the reflecting.

One significant conclusion I have come to is that it should be the person doing the reflecting who gets the most out of the experience. In order to manage this, they should have some ownership of the process, they should see and understand its purpose, and should not feel that it is something imposed upon them by others.

Why do we Need to Reflect?

One of the benefits of reflection is its impact on professionalism. Through reflecting on our practice, we become more aware, more in control, more able to see our strengths and development needs. Through reflection, we can begin to move from novice to expert. Berliner (2001: 5–13) states: 'To the novice the expert appears to have uncanny abilities to notice things, an "instinct" to make the right moves, an ineffable ability to get things done and to perform in an almost effortless manner' (in Banks and Mayes, 2001: 20).

He talks about the five stages: novice, advanced beginner, competent performer, proficient and then expert. He suggests that 'the experts have ... an intuitive grasp of the situation and a non-analytic and non-deliberative sense of the appropriate response to be made'. Berliner goes on to say:

> The wealth of knowledge and routines that they employ, in fact, is so automatic that they often do not realize why they performed a certain plan or action over another. However, when questioned, they are able to reconstruct the reasons for their decisions and behaviour. (In Banks and Mayes, 2001: 27)

It is this process, the questioning or self-questioning to reconstruct what happened – or to construct what might happen – that enables the teacher to move from novice to expert. Indeed, it helps the expert to continue to grow and develop. It may even enable the expert to pass on this expertise to other professionals as they share their reflections.

It is well documented that to develop as professionals we need to be able to reflect on our practice and to learn from this reflection. Donald Schön (1983) suggested that the capacity to reflect on action is to engage in the process of *continuous learning* and that this is one of the defining characteristics of professional practice.

What is Reflection?

There are many definitions of professionalism, and probably just as many definitions of reflection. It is important to establish what definitions I am using to underpin the ideas in this book.

There is much written about notions of professionalism. Authors such as Carr (2000), Sachs (2001) and Story and Hutchison (2001) view a professional as someone with training, expertise, autonomy and values consistent with the society of the time. For the purposes of this book, I will assume a shared acceptance of the 'training and expertise' aspects, but the values and autonomy perhaps require some discussion.

Professional values

It is important to acknowledge that being professional is about much more than 'what you do'. It is also about *how you do it* and the values that go along with it. It is about how you behave, it is about who you are and how you see yourself. Our actions and attitudes are influenced by our values and what we believe is 'right', 'just' and 'fair'. Often, we can become entrenched in our own view of the world and do not see some of the other 'possibilities'. Given the enormous influence we have on the lives of young people, it is important to be aware of how the values transmitted, either consciously or unconsciously, are appropriate. This book suggests that through talking about our profession, through articulating some of these deep-seated beliefs and values in terms of professional practice, we might begin to better understand them. Often, we do not realize that we hold some of these values until we have cause to stop and reflect upon what we did/said, why this might be and what effect this might have upon others in our care.

Teachers in particular can be very self-critical, and the demands of the profession are such that we often take even constructive criticism from others badly. We, nevertheless, blame ourselves for any seeming disaster that occurs in the course of our duties. Yet, on the other hand, we get little formal recognition for our victories and seldom stop to celebrate our expertise. It is often only when we stop and reflect that we realize how far we have come and how well we have done. This idea of reflection is not new. Many institutions have reflection embedded in the systems that operate in the professional environment. For many, it is this reflection and these values that help to define their professional identity.

Professional identity

Osgood (2006) suggests that 'a professional identity is performatively constituted, "being professional" is a performance, which is about what practitioners do at particular times, rather than a universal indication of who they are'.

This is echoed by Sachs (2003) who states that 'across society, professionalism increasingly refers to an individual's attitude and behaviour, rather than a group's formal status and collective identity'.

Without reflection, these elements may get locked away and development is hindered. Through reflecting on practice and on 'what it is to be professional' the door is opened to better understanding and potential development of the tools that will enable you to develop and grow professionally. These are tools that will support your practice in times of change, where attitudes and approaches must adapt and develop.

Reflective practice is specifically about reflecting on oneself and one's inner world, behaviours and impact. Therefore, we need to consider much more than performance. Many 'expert professionals' can operate well in difficult situations and not tell you how they did so. Through reflection and articulation, it is possible to learn how to express these things and to understand what made the difference in a certain situation. It is possible to look at your own beliefs and values and consider them in the light of your profession. The whole autonomy element of professionalism can only really be addressed if you are able to stop for a moment and reflect on your practice.

Donald Schön (1983) has written extensively on this relationship between reflection and professionalism. He states:

> A professional practitioner is a specialist who encounters certain types of situations again and again … He develops a repertoire of expectations. He learns what to look for … As long as his practice is stable, in the sense that it brings him the same types of cases he becomes less and less subject to surprise … As practice becomes more repetitive and routine … the practitioner may miss important opportunities to think about what he is doing. He may be drawn into patterns of error which he cannot correct … When this happens the practitioner has *over learned* what he knows.
>
> A practitioner's reflection can serve as a corrective to *over learning*. Through reflection he *can* surface and criticize the tacit understandings that have grown up around the repetitive experiences of a specialized practice, and can make new sense of the situation of uncertainty or uniqueness which he may allow

himself to experience … Sometimes he arrives at a new theory of the phenom-
enon by articulating a feeling he has about it … When someone reflects in
action, he becomes a researcher in the practice context. He does not separate
thinking from doing. (In Pollard, 2002: 6–7)

Professional expertise

Having trained and qualified to do your chosen profession, it is
important to realize that this is not the end of the journey. Becoming
a professional is not the end, merely a stop en route. The continuous
development – constantly developing and updating knowledge and
expertise – is what separates the professional from the technician.

Fullan (2007) suggests that every teacher has to learn, virtually every
day. I would contest this and suggest that it is not 'virtually' every
day, but indeed *every* single day! He goes on to state that 'to improve
we need to do two things: to measure ourselves and be open about
what we are doing'. The reflective process is one approach to this
challenge, and one I will discuss in more detail in the following chapters of this book.

Professional autonomy

There is, of course, a well-documented, ongoing debate about autonomy for professionals. There is always a fine balance between, on the
one hand, the need for results and accountability, and on the other,
the professional judgement and independent licence required to
respond to day-to-day situations.

Quicke (1998) argues that teachers can be moral leaders only if they
have sufficient autonomy to develop 'strategies and approaches in
ways which, in their view, will benefit society' (cited in Banks and
Mayes, 2001: 47). However, decades of government intervention
have led to the erosion of professional autonomy. In particular, for
teachers, 'the application of rigor, and of robust standards and pro-
cedures by successive governments, has widely been viewed as an
undermining of autonomy and creative potential in the classroom,
with teachers as ciphers, simply technicians of the process' (Storey
and Hutchison, 2001: 47).

Brown (1989) argues that 'teachers work spontaneously from their
own situations and this does not tally well with a more systematic,
define objectives – plan activities – evaluate achievement of objects,
approach'.

It is this spontaneity and autonomy that should be nurtured in order to maintain a true sense of professionalism. The aim of this book is to examine some of the ways that the professional might be able to develop self-awareness regarding their own skills, aptitudes and values, through a process based upon reflective practice.

Professional accountability

However, it would be wrong to argue for a generation of maverick individuals, each working from individual ideals and purposes. Of course, we need boundaries and guidelines. In Scotland, the GTCS (2008) believes that the Code of Professionalism and Conduct has achieved this. 'It also has the benefit of making the profession more secure in its own professional standards yet, at the same time, making it more accountable to the public.' The GTCS advises teachers that they have 'tried to balance producing a book of rules or an exhaustive list of "do's and don'ts" with the broader, less prescriptive approach of a Code. This is to assist and support the individual teacher in relation to the professional judgments he or she has to make on a day-to-day basis'.

Models of professionalism

Eraut (1994: 2) suggests two models for teacher professionalism: the 'functionalist model emphasises expertise and relative autonomy; the traditional model concerns restrictions for entry and *continuing competence* with adherence to a code and self-regulation'.

It is this continuing competence, the continuous professional development which drives the ideas in this book. 'Reflection is skilled practice that uses experience, knowledge and enquiry processes to increase our capability to intervene, interpret, and act positively on successes, problems, issues and significant questions' (Ghaye, 2011: 20).

Fullan (2008: 80) agrees: 'No part of the work of a consistent effective performance is static. In the midst of any action, there is a constant learning whether it consists of detecting and correcting common errors or discovering new ways to improve'.

Moon (2001: 365) argues that 'apparently, the most obvious reason for teachers to undergo work towards reflective practice is because teacher educators think it is a good thing'. This is echoed by Tabachnick and Zeicher (1991: 14, cited in Pollard, 2002: 14) where they suggest that 'neither Cruikshank nor Schön have much to say, for example, about what it is that teachers ought to be reflecting about ... the impression is given that as long as teachers are reflecting about something, in some manner, whatever they decide to do is all right since they have reflected about it'.

One of the aims of this book is to justify the development of reflective practice and open up the debate about what to do, how to do it and how to turn reflection into meaningful action and development for the professional. Above all, it is about meaningful self-initiated reflection where the reflector feels in control of the process and has ownership of the agendas. It needs to be so much more than a tick-box activity or a task completed to keep 'our masters' happy.

This process is described as:

> 'changing common sense thinkers', who are externally motivated to reflect, into 'pedagogical thinkers', who reflect habitually. (LaBoskey cited in Banks and Mayes, 2001: 366)

Professional reflection as action research

Richard Winter (2001) argues that 'practitioner action research is part of the general ideal of professionalism'. In addition to this, Elliot (1982) defines action research as: 'the study of a social situation with the view to improving the quality of action within it ... (The) total process – review, diagnosis, planning, implementation, monitoring effects – provides the necessary link between self-evaluation and professional development' (cited in Banks and Mayes, 2001: 297).

Tony Ghaye (2011), speaks in favour of collaborative research, and suggests that:

> Improvement cannot take place unless we learn from experience. Failure to do this is resigning ourselves to being prisoners to our past. Reflection-on-practice is an intentional action; the intention is to improve the quality of educational experiences through a rigorous reflection of the learning that has accrued as a consequence of engaging reflective practices of one kind or another. (Ghaye, 2011: 134)

As Clark and Peterson (1986: 37) suggest, 'Teachers are revealed as responsible, reflective professionals, whose theories and belief systems influence, to a large degree, their perceptions of classroom experiences and who thus monitor their thoughts and actions involved in the teaching process'. Thiessen (2001: 320) puts it neatly: 'Teachers learn from each other. They cite fellow teachers as the most valuable source of professional development.' The approach advocated in this book seeks to take advantage of this valuable resource as a means of facilitating professional development.

However, it cannot be assumed that because you are a good professional, you therefore reflect, nor that because you reflect you are therefore a good professional. Moon (2001) suggests that, perhaps the most important thing is the idea that the 'teacher as reflective practitioner will not happen simply because it is a good, or even compelling idea' (Moon, 1990: 69).

Professional reflection in initial teacher education

It is important, therefore, to explore the various ways in which reflection has been introduced, encouraged and formalized in order to evaluate its impact on developing professional practice.

Government initiatives

Recent government initiatives have tried to raise the status of this kind of reflection by integrating 'reflection' into the requirements for registration. In the Standard for Initial Teacher Education in Scotland, it describes one element of professionalism as: 'taking responsibility for and being committed to your own professional development arising from professional enquiry and reflection on your own and other professional practices' (GTCS, 2008, section 3.1).

In England, there is a similar emphasis placed on reflection. The QTS standards guidance Q7 (a) states that teachers should:

> Reflect on and improve their practice, and take responsibility for identifying and meeting their developing professional needs.
>
> In the context of new professionalism, teachers find themselves increasingly both developing their skills as coaches and mentors, and benefiting from the coaching and mentoring that they receive. (GTC, 2008 Rationale:1)

It goes on to state: 'This standard requires trainees to develop an ability to make judgements about the effectiveness of their teaching, and to identify ways of bringing about improvement.'

Here we have a clear steer in the direction of reflection. The fact that the requirements for qualification include such an approach does provide some justification for the ideas in this book. However, beyond that, there is the idea that we remember best the things we learn for ourselves; we learn best when we feel motivated, in control, with some sense of ownership and purpose to our learning. These elements suggest that despite any external pressures, reflection can be a very useful, powerful, supportive and motivational influence in our professional development.

What is reflection?

Bolton (2010: 13) said that: 'Reflective practice is learning through examining what we think happened on any occasion, and how we think others perceived the event and us, opening our practice to scrutiny by others.'

> Length of experience does not automatically confer insight and wisdom. Ten years of experience can be one year's worth of distracted experiences repeated ten times.

She then goes on to suggest that

> Reflection becomes critical when it has two distinct purposes. The first is to understand how considerations of power undergrid, frame and distort educational processes and interactions. The second is to question assumptions and practices that seem to make our teaching lives easier but academically work against our best interests. (Brookfield, 1995: 7–8)

It is this improvement that is essential to the reflection. It is not enough merely to reflect.

> A generalization that seems to apply to teaching, is the fact that there is relatively little concern for the effect of reflective practice on the subject of the professional's action ... Since the improvement in learning is deemed central to the purposes of these professions, this seems to be a surprising omission ... Copeland, Birmingham and Lewin (1993: 247–59) ask a critical question: 'Do students of highly reflective teachers learn more or better or even differently?' (Moon, 1999)

In 2000, the GTC in England stated: 'The focus for the early years of professional development should be on engaging the individual teacher in reflection and action on pedagogy, the quality of learning, setting targets and expectations, equal opportunities, planning, assessment and monitoring, curriculum and subject knowledge, and classroom knowledge' (GTC, 2000 rationale p1). There is a strong lead here to what we should be reflecting upon and what kind of action we might take as a result of this reflection.

However, reflecting on practice, after the event, is a luxury that most teachers say they cannot afford. Ask in any staffroom and the response will be, 'When?'. With all the pressures and requirements of the modern classroom, teachers do not need more 'distractions'. Talk to them about reflection and they will tell you that they do indeed reflect all the time. But the reflection of a seasoned professional takes place *in* practice, *on* the job. Indeed for some, this takes the form of 'firefighting', of reacting to the things that are not working. Adapting, adjusting, responding – all are already done in practice: professionals instinctively develop practice. Why then the need for a formal approach? Why more bureaucracy? If it is about reflection, whose reflection are we talking about? Is it imposed, contrived, something to deliver an agenda, owned by someone else, or has it some purpose and benefit for those taking part?

Wildman and Niles observed that systematic reflection on teaching required a sound ability to understand classroom events in an objective manner (in Banks and Mayes, 2001: 364). They suggest that teachers rarely have the time or opportunities to view their own teaching or the teaching of others in an objective manner. Further observation revealed the tendency of teachers to evaluate events rather than review the contributory factors in a considered manner – in effect, standing outside the situation or progressing to the higher levels of reflection in terms of Van Manen's model (Van Manen, 1991).

Reflecting *in* practice is a skill that develops as we progress from novice to expert in our profession. Initially, there will be careful planning, supplemented by more than a little 'fire fighting', as things do not go as expected and adaptations need to be made. At such times reflection takes place. However, this reflection is not articulated, and is partly an unconscious 'survival' instinct, to get us through the experience.

Taken *in* practice, during the event, it is at least honest, useful, acted upon and 'vital'. *After* the event, if it happens at all, it is more about the past than the future. It might be a brief glance over the shoulder, a hope that tomorrow different mistakes will be made. Often, it's buried in the belief that there is no time for dwelling on the lessons of the past. Yet, when it is possible to stop and reflect, when perhaps there is someone to listen, then there is the opportunity to learn from an experience, to look towards the future with new insight. Surely, this is what reflection is meant to be about?

Experienced professionals will say that early difficulties are soon forgotten, that teaching becomes a second instinct and the process of reflecting, adjusting and so on also become second nature. However, if teachers can make these adjustments without seeming to think about them, are they truly reflecting? Will these 'on the job' adjustments initiate real change, or will they simply perpetuate many of the same difficulties? And what of the values that underpin the actions? Is there space here for such considerations? After all, it is these values which underpin what we do and how we do it.

Much better then to stop for a moment, to take stock, to articulate what is happening and to work out the reasons why. We move on then, from the particular incident to the more general policy and pedagogy, where consideration produces real change, where practice is transformed. This is where reflection, articulation and theory come together to provide 'institutional change'.

However, this skill does not come overnight. Professional reflection, being encouraged to stop and take stock of what happened, and why it happened, can help to develop this professional instinct in a much less haphazard way. It is well known that it is *experience*, and not *years in post* that gives professionals the best resource on which to draw. That experience is most valuable, and its benefit most palpable, when some kind of reflection takes place. Better still if such reflection is articulated and acted upon in some way. As Elizabeth Bird puts it, 'where a teacher makes a change to her practice as a result of this process, the next step is evaluation of the impact on her practice' (Bird, 2001: 290). There are a number of models which strive to encourage reflection and its impact on practice, and I will outline the traditional models before outlining the main approach advocated in this book.

Traditional models

Traditionally, reflection is very closely bound up with assessment, evaluation and accountability. The reflection is there to provide evidence to the person doing the assessing. The reflection itself is the manifestation of thinking and learning, and this is shared with the person who has the authority to make judgement and supply support. In the past, this has been bound to some form of written reflective paper, or, more recently, on observation and feedback.

Observation and feedback in ITE

In ITE, the tutor would go into a school and observe the trainee teacher in class. This would be followed by a discussion where the tutor would try to elicit reflective comments from the student which sum up, justify or expose their ideas, approaches and values. This opportunity to discuss practice and justify approaches has many benefits. However, it also puts a good deal of pressure on the participants, and a lot of significance on a one-off situation where the lesson and feedback take place.

In Scotland, it was found that the discussion was often tainted by the very act of assessment. The feedback comments, both oral and written, were lost under the weighty significance of the grade given. It was the grade and not the formative comments that were the focus. Students were most interested in the A grade, or the D. Tutors were often preoccupied to 'justify the grade' in their feedback.

In recent years, there has been a move away from this approach. Informed by the findings of Black and Williams (2002) and Shirley Clarke (2003), the grade approach has been replaced by a simple satisfactory/unsatisfactory mark: thus enabling the oral and written feedback to be formative and represent a positive look forward to what the student can do to improve in the future. However, there still exists the imbalance of power between the person reflecting on their practice and the supporter who is more knowledgeable and has more power and authority. Such a model of reflection gives the reflector little sense of autonomy or freedom to experiment and develop. Indeed, it may inhibit reflection if the reflector feels that honest reflection might be judged to be inadequate for a successful outcome to the interaction.

Part of teacher training is concerned with trying to develop reflexive practice and reflective practitioners. Within the ITE institutions, there are mechanisms to encourage students to reflect upon their teaching and learning experiences. These tend to take the form of conversations with an 'expert', be it a tutor or classroom practitioner. One of the difficulties with this is that the students themselves do not 'own' the agenda. They have some reflection, but this tends to be based on the requirements of the course for them to meet certain criteria. They also have the driving need to 'be successful', or at least to appear to be successful. This is not entirely conducive with someone being totally honest and prepared to admit what their heartfelt reflections might be.

What this book is about is something quite different. The best and most significant reflection is that which is self-motivated. The only agenda involved is that of the person trying to make sense of their own learning, and wanting to make things better. It has little to do with 'passing the course', or even with getting a 'high grade'. It is about learning and having a disposition to learn continuously.

What is the Impact on Practice?

This discussion about reflection is all very well, but it is important to remember that it should be taking us somewhere, otherwise it is going to be lost in all the other activities associated with the teaching profession. Reflection needs to have some impact. This impact should be such that it leads you to progress in your understanding, expertise or practice. It might lead you to then go out to search for informed views through your professional reading. It might prompt you to develop practice through experimenting with your own peda-gogy. It might prompt you to seek support from a peer, a colleague or a 'more experienced' professional.

One way or another, the reflection needs to have some impact on the learning of the person reflecting, or on the learning of those in their care. Therefore, there needs to be some kind of action that follows this reflection. This is something that will be discussed further in Chapter 5.

 Summary

In this chapter, we looked at professionalism and how it is defined. We explored the significance of professional reflection in the development of skills, attitudes and values. We also explored the link between reflec-tion and professionalism and how the two elements support each other. We then looked at some of the benefits and challenges associ-ated with regular professional reflection. Different ways of supporting and encouraging reflection were evaluated. Finally, we considered the importance of the link between reflection and the impact on practice.

Focus Reflection Questions

It is customary in books such as this to ask the reader to reflect on their learning. However, this is generally considered as a personal reflection, done in isolation, without a need to articulate in any way the reaction to the focus questions. In order to be consistent with the philosophy espoused by the book, I suggest that this reflection is articulated, ideally with a peer who is also engaged in this study. Below are some focus questions to consider. If possible, get someone else to take on the role of enabler: asking the questions but not putting forward their own views, enabling you to think about, reflect on and articulate your own thoughts first. This should be your first experience of having a 'professional monologue', where you have the opportunity to articulate your thinking safe from judgement or interruption.

〰 Questions for Reflection

- What experience have you had of being required to reflect on your own performance/understanding?
- Who did you feel was making the decisions about what to discuss?
- To what extent were you wary of expressing your true feelings?
- To what extent did you feel like the other person was really listening and was interested in your progress?
- What is your view of the idea that there could be reflection which is your own: your own agenda, your own opportunity to explore your own development and understanding – free from any sense of judgement or criticism?
- Discuss a recent occasion where you reflected in practice, where you reflected on practice after the event, and where you reflected in a manner that enabled you to have an impact on the next steps for you as a professional.
- Read through and look out for definitions of reflection and professionalism.
- Consider whether the approaches discussed suggest encouragement for the reflection to be open and honest, genuine reflection.
- Consider whether the scenarios discussed do in fact overcome the possible challenges of a power imbalance between participants.
- Consider whether there is, nevertheless, still a danger of imposed agendas or contrived reflection.
- Consider other arguments, not presented here, that the more traditional modes of reflection presented in the readings still have much to offer in supporting professional reflection.

Further Reading

- Browne, A. and Haylock, D. (2004) *Professional Issues for Primary Teachers*. London: Sage.
- Cohen, L., Manion, K. and Morrison, K. (2011) *Research Methods in Education*, 7th edn. London: Routledge.
- Englund, T. (2004) 'The modern teacher constructed on different arenas', Paper presented at The European Conference of Educational Research University of Crete, 22–25 September.
- Everton, T., Turner, P., Hargreaves, L. and Pell, T. (2000) 'Public perceptions of the teaching profession', *Research Papers in Education*, 22 (3): 247–66.
- Hodkinson, P. (1997) 'Neo-Fordism and teacher professionalism', *Teacher Development*, 1: 69–82.
- Mayes, A.S. (2001) 'National Standards for teachers: twenty-first century possibilities for professional development', in Banks, F. and Shelton Mayes, A. (eds), *Early Personal Development for Teachers*. London: David Fulton/The Open University.

References

Banks, F. and Shelton Mayes, A. (eds) (2001) *Early Professional Development for Teachers*. London: David Fulton/The Open University, pp 41–53.

Berliner D.C. (2001) 'Teacher expertise', in Banks, F. and Shelton Mayes, A. (eds), *Early Professional Development for Teachers*. London, David Fulton/The Open University, pp 20–26.

Bird, E. (2001) 'The classroom teacher and school-based research', in Banks, F. and Shelton Mayes, A. (eds), *Early Professional Development for Teachers*. London: David Fulton/The Open University, pp 273–296.

Black, P., Harrison, C., Lee, C., Marshall, B. and Wiliam, D. (2002) *Working Inside the Black Box*. London: King's College.

Bolton, G. (2010) *Reflective Practice*, 3rd edn. London: Sage.

Brookfield, S. (1995) *Becoming a Critically Reflective Teacher*. San Francisco: Jossey-Bass.

Brown, S. A. (1989) 'How do teachers talk about and evaluate their own teaching?', *Spotlight 12*. Edinburgh: Scottish Council for Educational Research.

Carr, D. (2000) *Professionalism and Ethics in Teaching*. London: Routledge.

Clark and Peterson (1986) 'Teachers' thought processes', in Wittrock 'Implications for teacher education', *Journal of Teacher Education*, 37(5), 27–31.

Cohen, L. and Manion, L. (2011) *Research Methods in Education*, 7th edn. London: Routledge.

Copeland, W., Birmingham, C. and Lewin, B. (1993) 'The reflective practitioner in teaching: towards a research agenda', *Teaching and Teacher Education*, 9 (4): 247–59.

Elliot, J. (1982) 'Action reseacher: a framework for self-evaluation in schools'. Working paper No.1, p. ii, p1, Teacher-Pupil Interaction and the Quality of Learning. London: Schools Council (mimeo).

Englund, T. (2004) 'The modern teacher constructed on different arenas'. Paper presented at the European Conference on Educational Research, University of Crete, 22–25 September.

Eraut, M. (1994) *Developing Professional Knowledge and Competence*. London, available at: http://www.tandfonline.com/doi/full/10.1080/158037042000225245

Everton, T., Galton, M. and Pell, T. (2000) 'Teachers' perspectives on educational research: knowledge and content' *Journal of Education for Teaching*, 26 (2): 168–82.

Fullan, M. (2008) *The Six Secrets of Change: What the Best Leaders Do to Help Their Organizations Survive and Thrive*. Chichester: John Wiley & Sons.

General Teaching Council for Scotland (2006) *Standard for Initial Teacher Education. Core Professional Interests*, 3.1. http://www.gtcs.org.uk/standards/standard-initial-teacher-education.aspx.

Ghaye, T. (2011) *Teaching and Learning through Reflective Practice: a Practical Guide for Positive Action*, 2nd edn. Oxen: Routledge.

GTC (2000) General Teaching Council. *Countinuing Professional Development: Advice to Government*. London: GTC. See Rationale, p1 http://media.education.gov.uk/assets/files/pdf/q/qts%20standards%20guidance%2/0q7a.pdf

LaBoskey, V. (1993) 'A conceptual framework for reflection in pre-service teacher education', in Calderhead, J. and Gates, P. (eds) *Conceptualising Reflection in Teacher Development*. London: Falmer Press.

Moon, J. (1999) *Reflection in Learning and Professional Development*. Kogan Page Limited, reprinted by RoutledgeFalmer, Oxen, England.

Moon, J. (2001) 'Learning through reflection', in Banks, F. and Shelton Mayes, A. (eds) *Early Professional Development for Teachers*. London: David Fulton/The Open University, pp 27.

Oja, S. N. (1989) 'Teachers: ages and stages of adult development', in Holly, M. L. and McLoughlin, C.S. (eds) *Perspectives on Teacher Professional Development*. Lewes: Falmer Press.

Osgood, J. (2006) 'Deconstructing professionalism in early childhood education: resisting the resultory gaze', *Contemporary Issues in Early Childhood*, 7, 1. http://londonmet.academia.edu/JayneOsgood/papers/377860/Deconstructing_professionalism_In_Early_childhood_Education_resisting_the_Regulatory_Gaze.

Rollett, B. A. (2001) 'How do expert teachers view themselves?', in Banks, F. and Shelton Mayes, A. (eds) *Early Professional Development for Teachers*. London: David Fulton/The Open University, pp 27–40.

Schön, D. (2002) 'Reflection-in-action', in Pollard, A. (ed) *Readings for Reflective Teaching*. London: Continuum, page 7. Edited from Schön, D.A. (1983) *The Reflective Practitioner: How Professionals think in Action*. London: Temple Smith, pp. 50–68.

Storey, A. and Hutchison, S. (2001) 'The meaning of teacher professionalism in a quality control era', in Banks, F. and Shelton Mayes, A. (eds) *Early Professional Development for Teachers*. London: David Fulton/The Open University, pp. 41–53.

Tabachinick, R. and Zeichner, K. (2002) 'Reflections on reflective teaching', in Pollard, A. (ed) *Readings for Reflective Teaching*. Continuum, London, p 14.

Thiessen, D. (2001), 'Classroom-based teacher development', in Banks, F. and Shelton Mayes, A. (eds) *Early Professional Development for Teachers*. London: David Fulton/The Open University, pp 17–331.

Van Manen, M. (1991) *The Tact of Teaching*. New York: The State of New York Press, p 35.

Wenger, E. (2006) 'Communities of practice: A brief introduction', Available at: http://www.ewenger. Com/theory/communities_of_Practice_intro: htm

Wildman, R. and Niles, J. (1987) 'Reflective teachers: tension between abstractions and realities', *Journal of Teacher Education* 3, 25–31.

Winter, R. (1987) *Action Research and the Nature of Social Enquiry.* Aldershot: Gower Publishing.

Winter, R. (2001) 'Action reasearch as a professional ideal', in Banks, F. and Shelton Mayes, A. (eds) *Early Professional Development for Teachers.* London: David Fulton/The Open University, pp 297–299.

2

What Does Reflective Practice Look Like?

Chapter Overview

In this chapter, we will look at different approaches to reflective practice: looking at their purpose and their strengths and weaknesses. From general, incidental reflection, to highly organized management-initiated reflection, we will look at a wide range of approaches that have been explored over the last few decades. This chapter will also look at the role played by the person reflecting and the person 'supporting' this reflection: looking at issues of power, accountability and support. We will look at the benefits to both the professionals involved in the reflective interaction and evaluate the advantages of 'sharing' in these reflections. This chapter will also include some recent research into the concept of the reflective practitioner, and the way reflection is currently encouraged in practice. Finally, I will propose a different way of approaching reflection through using more of a 'counselling' approach: developing articulated learning through professional monologues.

> There is an increasing emphasis developing and sustaining an interrogatory approach that fosters innovation and enhancement of professional practices. Reflection has to be purposeful and rigorous and take on a critical dimension in order to bring about change. (Forde and O' Brien, 2011: 29)

- Different forms of reflection
- Initial teacher educational and reflective portfolios
- Mentoring
- Management-initiated reflection

- Opportunities to work with a peer
- Incidental and anecdotal professional reflection
- Models of reflection
- Professional monologues
- A counselling approach
- Other considerations

Different Forms of Reflection

General reflection and pro formas

Most professions have mechanisms to encourage reflection in some form or another. In teaching, staff have long been encouraged to evaluate their teaching and the impact of their lessons. However, this has mostly been pupil-orientated and to do with the short term 'here and now' rather than a more in-depth analysis regarding what can be learned about oneself as a teacher and learner.

Many authorities have pro formas to structure reflection, though this approach is patchy and generally structured to support a professional review and development (PRD) consultation, which, at best, might be undertaken only once a year. Such meetings tend to be more focused on the career development of the teacher than on the specifics of how they are performing on a day-to-day basis. In fact, it is debatable whether or not the PRD process is about professional reflection at all. Certainly, it provides management with opportunities to work with staff to establish strengths and development needs. However, it is generally viewed as the title suggests – as a review. The review of a year, looking back at how far you have travelled professionally, is indeed a worthy aim. However, the opportunity to focus in detail on things that went well and to begin to 'unpack' what didn't, isn't possible in such encounters. Cynical critics would suggest that, in fact, the PRD process is more about managerial control and appraisal than a supportive, developmental reflection process.

In other professions, there will be equivalent structures to facilitate reviews of progress, but again these tend to be more of an annual review than a focused analysis of professional practice.

Initial Teacher Education and Reflective Portfolios

In Initial Teacher Education, students are encouraged to reflect frequently and in a systematic manner. Within most faculties in

Scotland, they are encouraged to maintain a reflective portfolio, tracking their own personal learning journey. This portfolio attempts to introduce personal and professional reflection, which in turn creates a foundation upon which personal development can be built. This formal approach to reflection is a good starting point.

This kind of approach is described as having the aim of developing critical and reflective practice, where practitioners are able to assess strengths and weaknesses in order to improve their practice. The professional portfolio is fundamentally a map, with a brief reflective narrative of progress, that will support students to meet the requirements of the Standard for Initial Teacher Education.

Benefits of keeping a portfolio

- It enables you to take increasing responsibility and ownership for your own professional development.

- It helps you internalize a process of professional learning as a basis for continuing professional development in your teaching career.

- It encourages you to express how your prior experiences and knowledge have influenced you and continue to contribute to your professional development.

- It offers the opportunity to describe, analyse, explain and reflect on your developing understanding of the links between theory and practice as part of a professional community of practice.

- It encourages you to identify links between school placement and university learning.

- It has the potential of providing information on your achievements in the programme and will offer a sound basis for completion of the final profile into the teaching profession.

- It connects with the responsibility you will have as a probationer in compiling a Probationer Professional Development Portfolio.

Mentoring

Student placement

Out in schools on placement, students are encouraged to reflect on specific lessons and sequences. Again, the approach is to stop and consider what can be learned from an experience: what can be learned about the approach, the content, the impact and, of course, what can you learn about yourself. This introduction is a good start, though one might question the solitary nature of it. Is it really enough to encourage students to merely raise the questions? And how can we know if they are asking the right questions? It would still be too easy to produce a paper which contains 'contrived reflection' – a mock analysis, which is the result of a sense of obligation to fulfil *someone else's* agenda.

Tutor visits

Students do have some support in reflection via the tutor visit from the Initial Teacher Institute or University. However, in some parts of the UK this has been affected by lack of funding and by changes in government approaches. The whole system is currently in question at the moment in Scotland, with suggestions about increased partnership between schools and universities, with schools being given more and more of the responsibility, and with the ITE institutions being involved in the school itself less and less. Some of the ideas in this book might be one way of supporting these changes and of supporting the learners and their mentors.

Certainly, there is no dispute that support for professional development from a more experienced mentor is invaluable. Students benefit greatly from the feedback given by tutors visiting them on placement. A critical view while you are in practice can provide the most valuable and pertinent advice. On the other hand, the tutor visit often represents a one-off snapshot from someone the student does not know well, who is 'parachuted' in to make a judgement on practice. The result can be very nervous students producing below-par examples of practice, often accompanied by a class of pupils happy to exploit the situation and become uncharacteristically challenging in a manner which compounds the agony for the poor student. The visit is also affected by the knowledge that it is assessed and that for the student success is the main focus of the visit. In these circumstances, any kind of supportive formative feedback can be overshadowed by the big question, 'Yes, but did I pass?' There is also the financial burden on supplying quality supervision for students on placement. Such visits are time-consuming and expensive to maintain. Indeed, many universities are cutting back on the provision and looking for alternative methods of supporting and assessing students on placement.

Mentors

In comparison with the student–tutor relationship, the relationship between mentor and student has the potential to be more support-ive of developing professional reflection. The mentor generally has had some sort of training and is given time to support and advise their student. This is true, not just in the teaching profession, but in other professions too. The mentor has the student's best interests at heart and there is the scope for an effective, constructive professional relationship to develop. The mentor will see more of the day-to-day practice so that the snapshot argument has less validity. The nerves of the tutor visit and unpredictable classroom behaviour under pres-sure will also be less of an issue for observation between mentor and student.

The mentor has the opportunity to support and develop profes-sional practice with the student over a period of time and any judgements will be tempered by an in-depth knowledge of the circumstances of the context. However, it is important to acknowl-edge that a mentor has a very challenging set of priorities to balance, and the desire to enable their protégé to succeed can have a nega-tive impact on true professional reflection. They may interpret the requirements for success in ways that put pressure on a more responsive approach to reflection.

Mentors may still lean heavily on a set agenda, a structure which *directs* reflection rather than supports it. There is also still the situa-tion where the 'expert' supports the 'novice', and all the implications of power and obligation that surround such a context.

Then there are the 'reluctant' mentors, who are not in fact in the role out of professional benevolence, but are instead press-ganged into the supporting role and perhaps less than committed to it. In such circumstances, the student is left to 'the luck of the draw' and may have to develop despite, rather than because of, the mentor support.

Probation/induction

Once qualified, students move on to their probation. They will still have fellow professionals to support them, but again the arguments above will exist in the kind of support and the significance of the kind of relationship they have. The experience for the fledgling will depend very much on the skill, experience and approach of the mentor.

Mentors in school

Often, during their probationary period, students may be supported by an official mentor. The mentor, working in school, is there to encourage and support reflection. For the developing teacher, this affords a supportive 'critical friend' to help them to look at their developing practice. For the mentor, there is also much benefit; they too are put in a situation where reflection is a regular and structured experience.

The work done between mentor and emerging professional is extremely valuable. Training is provided for both players and a clear structure exists for reflective practice to take place. Generally, the format for this is the traditional 'observation and feedback' model, which is also used in initial teacher education and in many local authorities. The advantage of this is that the reflective discussion can focus on what happens in the classroom and what impact this reflection might have on future practice. One disadvantage is that the 'learner' is dependent on their relationship with the mentor, and confined, to some extent, by their values and judgement. The 'learner' will also have that feeling of being *judged*. How honest should their reflection be, given that the audience is the same as the assessor of their success? There is also the problem that, having seen the lesson, any subsequent questions will appear 'loaded' to the anxious apprentice awaiting feedback. One of the ideas promoted by this book is that, if this is the tone of the mentoring relationship, how can authentic professional reflection take place if it is always in the shadow of an assessment agenda?

The suggestions in this book are designed to support both the emerging professional and the experienced practitioner in having a positive professional encounter where there is benefit to both parties, but where the agenda for learning is firmly in the hands of the one doing most of the learning.

In a study into student perceptions of tutor feedback, Stevens and Lowing (2008: 162–98) reported that:

> Beginning student teachers displayed a general feeling of anxiety about the manner in which their tutor might assess their lessons, especially early in teaching practice. This anxiety tended to focus on the nature of the feedback they would receive from their tutor, and the unpredictability – and its inevitable repercussions – of the observed class's mood when the tutor was present in the lesson … students did not want to be 'caught on a bad day with an awful class'.

This book seeks to explore how this relationship can be improved. The approach provides a tool to support this very valuable interaction between mentor and 'learner'.

However, the approach is based upon the principle that we remember best what we learn for ourselves, and that if we can only get away from the notion of 'imposed reflection', and of 'someone else's agenda', then we can be free from the inhibitions that possible judgement and criticism might bring.

Management-initiated Reflection

Well-meaning as it may sound, reflection can be perceived as threatening when its only oxygen is provided through a management structure, such as a professional review meeting once a year. Many institutions have programmes of professional review and development, or professional review and appraisal. Whatever they are called, they strive to achieve seemingly contradictory aims. On the one hand, they seek to encourage reflection on professional practice. They encourage and structure professionals to stop and consider their own practice and performance. On the other hand, they also serve to inform those in authority about the performance of staff, enabling them to make some evaluation of how well staff are performing and establish where improvement might be required. In some settings, this can be a very supportive and helpful encounter. Professionals reflect on their practice, seek support and discuss development paths. In return, the person in authority listens, documents progress and offers development opportunities to enable the professional to continue to develop their practice in the future. In other settings, the appraisal element provides an opportunity for management to assess and share their evaluation of the professional's practice. For both scenarios, the person reflecting will be wary of the outcome and the impression that they might give. It is unlikely that they will be opening themselves up to criticism or admitting to too many difficulties. It is likely instead that they will be more cautious and guarded. For many professionals, these encounters have much less to do with reflection and much more to do with accountability and paper trails.

This kind of approach signals to the person reflecting that there is a management agenda, and that some reflection is required leading to a clear development strategy (often management-driven). Such an approach is a long way from the ideals of a self-initiated, self-imposed and acted-upon reflection. It would not be surprising if, in these circumstances, staff merely offerred 'development needs' that they thought management wanted to hear, or if they offered 'small attainable development needs', rather than properly engaging with what they really want and need to develop.

Of course, management have every right to suggest areas for improvement. It is their important role to encourage and support the development of their staff. They are the best people for understanding how authority and school agendas for improvement might be achieved.

However, I do not want us to confuse these two very different things. 'Professional reflection' is a personal thing. It should be a personal reflection with a personal agenda for improvement. This can then be shared in order to make sense of it and to gain advice and support. It is a look back at what has been, and at the same time a look forward to how things might be. It is about development that is personal and pertinent to the individual. It is possibly quite different from an authority, or school-led, development plan. Such plans are more oriented towards bigger, more general goals. These might or might not relate to the kind of (often more pressing) personal goals and priorities that an individual professional might have. Of course ideally, there will be some connection, some relationship between personal goals and corporate ones. However, the mechanisms for such joined-up thinking are not yet well established.

There is a place for both of these aspects of reflection in our development, but the one focused on in this book is the aspect that deals with personal self-selected development, based on independent reflection.

Opportunities to Work with a Peer

One way of developing personal professional reflection is through working with a peer. There are many advantages of this, as we often do need to articulate something in order to make sense of it. Working with a peer would suggest a positive move away from feelings of 'being judged', which come with management-led reflection. Also, having two players at roughly the same stage of development would surely provide a more level playing field.

Some justification for a peer learning approach comes from Boud et al. (1999):

1. Peer learning necessarily involves students working together and developing skills of collaboration. This gives them practice in planning and teamwork and involves them as part of a learning community in which they have a stake.

2. There are increased possibilities for students to engage in reflection and exploration of ideas when the authority of the teacher is not an immediate presence.

   'The general goal of collaborative learning is to replace the alienating, teacher-dominated methods of traditional instruction. Some students work best in the absence of authority'. (Annett, 1997)

Without denying these advantages, I will return to this later when I look at how collaboration and reflection can go together to enable effective professional articulation.

Incidental and Anecdotal Professional Reflection

All professionals reflect. It is an aspect of practice that they cannot ignore. However, it is the articulation of these reflections that will crystallize their thoughts into future action. Calderwood and Shorrock consider the key principle that: 'Student teachers learn a great deal about practice through talking about it, and often become more aware of aspects of their own practice as a result of such discussion. Talking about practice can also help student teachers clarify their vision of how they would like to teach' (Calderwood and Shorrock, 1997: 200).

Working with a peer is one way of introducing some structure to this process. Many staff will tell you that they reflect all the time. In order to survive at all, they must reflect *on* the job. Modifying and adapting plans; reacting to events and responses; and thinking on their feet, are all important skills of the seasoned professional.

Whilst reflections during practice are often essential in order to survive at all, reflecting *after* the event is less pressing and can be put aside on account of there always being more demanding 'active' things to do to take things forward. Consequently, we may keep doing the same things and getting the same kind of results.

If things do not go to plan, we would generally always reflect, if only in order not to make the same mistake again. However, in reflecting on what went well, or reflecting about what we learn about ourselves as professionals, this quality of reflection perhaps needs a little more structure. The dilemma is gaining the structure to achieve the quality of reflection without then causing it to feel imposed or contrived.

Certainly, professionals do reflect and share this reflection incidentally with colleagues. However, it tends to be throwaway comments over the photocopier or over coffee. It often has a focus on relationships or behaviour management issues. 'Too embarrassed to talk about your successes, too ashamed to talk about the failures, you end up just joining in with a moan about the class behaviour and not really going any further forward' (primary school teacher). Inevitably, it can become an opportunity for anecdotal offloading, with the person initiating the conversation feeling upstaged by those responding with a response along the lines of 'You were lucky, you should have seen what happened to me'.

What is required is some kind of agreement that, having begun this sharing of reflection, the stage is there – open and uninterrupted. The opportunity needs to exist where the professional is able and willing to articulate, free from comment, interruption and judgement, in order to make sense and opportunity out of these reflections. The challenge is how to set this up. Where do we find the time? How do we create the supportive ethos for this to work?

Models of Reflection

When considering the traditional approaches to 'reflection *on* practice', most models are based on the notion that the teacher is observed and then some kind of conversation is held in order to encourage reflection. There are various ways in which this is done.

- Authority figure and subject

- A tutor–tutee approach

- Mentor and 'learner'

- Learning rounds

- Lesson study

- a coaching model

Authority figure and subject

It is clear that in any profession there is a need for monitoring progress and the quality of performance. Traditionally, this is done by the person in authority observing the subject and, after the event, discussing the performance and supplying 'feedback'. 'This generally positive relationship is also characterised by a certain tension: the relationship between formative, developmental aspects of the tutor's role, and the rather more hard-edged evaluative and authoritative function' (Stevens and Lowing, 2008: 162–98).

In the past, this has often been a contentious issue, with the subject feeling 'judged', and the manner in which the person in authority has communicated their assessment has come in for some criticism. Recent inspections by Ofsted and HMIE have resulted in a good deal of stress in schools to the extent that they have now pulled back in their approach, trying to provide a more sensitive response to their observations.

In schools there has long been resistance to the head teacher sitting in on classes and then commenting on the 'performance' of staff – as opposed to providing positive and constructive feedback. In more recent times, this practice has been realigned to try to accommodate a more formative element so that it is less threatening and less judgemental. Nowadays, it is more likely to be represented as a supportive, staff development experience where observations take a single focus approach, with the subject agreeing in advance what will be discussed after the observation. However, there is still a good deal of suspicion regarding such observations. Even with the appearance of collaboration, it is always going to be difficult when the discussion has the imbalance in power and where there is an agenda, either an authority or school improvement agenda, or a management or personal one.

There are many challenges to this element of reflection. Head teachers and managers do not have the time and resources to complete observation and feedback often enough for it to represent useful professional development through reflection. There is no authentic link between reflection and these infrequent encounters between management and staff. Above all, there remains the fact that one partner in these encounters has much more power and authority over the other and so any kind of honest and open personal reflection is always going to be somewhat inhibited.

One way of approaching these encounters is to somehow give more of the agenda to the person reflecting instead of using them as a mere assessment tool.

> The common practice of observation and feedback which mentors are usually encouraged to undertake seems to miss an opportunity for supporting the informed participation of student teachers in the community of practice of teaching. Indeed, observation and feedback frequently operate as a system for monitoring the extent to which student teachers have adhered to their lesson plans, and have not been distracted by unanticipated pupil needs. (Edwards et al., 2002: 110)

If we can step away from assessment and judgement for a while, perhaps we can enable students and professionals to stop and reflect on their own terms, safe from the fear and anxiety of being judged or pushed into discussing the agendas and priorities of others, when they feel that they have much more pressing needs and concerns of their own.

A tutor–tutee approach

Initial teacher training has long worked on the principle of students being supported in their development by a tutor. The tutor is generally someone with expert knowledge, working in the university, or someone with a good deal of direct experience in the field, for example a retired head teacher. When on placement, the student will be visited by the tutor and the observation/feedback process will be conducted. This approach is similar to the one discussed above. The expert, acting as gatekeeper to the profession, will monitor standards and supply formative feedback, thus enabling the student to work on developing and honing their professional skills.

Not so long ago, the tutor would give out grades to signify how well the student had done. This of course was a very subjective practice and performance was often very much affected by the context and extent of the student's nerves at the time. More recently, the grading system ceased in Scotland and the approach has more of a 'supportive development needs' feel about it. However, there will always be the spectre of failure lurking in post-observation reflections and this can get in the way of genuine productive reflection.

Obviously, there is a need for judgements to be made. The standard and quality of performance needs to be monitored, improved and maintained. However, my feeling is that this needs to be kept separate from the process of personal professional reflection. There are times when the latter can feed into the former, but it is highly unlikely to work the other way round – judgement is unlikely to contribute to long-term cultural change of practice whereas genuine reflection can, and does, make all the difference.

Mentor and 'learner'

Perhaps the greatest hope for long-term cultural change is the new blood coming into teaching. Newly qualified teachers are given a mentor who has the role of 'expert' taking them through some of the details of what it is to be a professional. One aspect of this is the notion of reflection.

Whilst the standard of mentor will vary, there are excellent training schemes for these teachers to develop their own practice in order to support their new colleagues. Observation is still a part of the process of support and development. Again, a focused observation discussion is agreed between the two players. However, there is a good deal of variety in the quality of relationship between mentor and trainee. There will still be a sense of novice needing advice from expert, and with this the sense of novice being judged by expert. Skilled mentors can allay fears by developing strong relationships of mutual trust. They can enable trainees to work openly and honestly with them, so that reflection is authentic and productive. However, there are still those who struggle to relate in a manner which enables appropriate reflection and development to take place. There will always be an element of a power relationship where one person looks to the other for advice and answers; where one person has the knowledge, experience and power to influence the other. With such distractions, authentic professional reflection will be difficult to sustain and often the pressures of 'getting the job done' can interfere with working things out for yourself.

It may be that the approach advocated in this book will be of benefit to both categories.

Learning rounds and reflective practice

Learning rounds have been introduced in many Scottish schools recently. Based on the medical model of learning rounds, this is an approach which claims to encourage reflection and collegiality, and facilitate effective change across the school or authority. It is based on an approach where observers create a base of evidence which *describes* what they have seen. One of its strengths is that there are no evaluative comments or value-laden points. The team will observe and then discuss how they, their school or authority will use the data to bring about improvement.

> This evidence-based process leads to a continuous development of practice at personal, school and authority level. Staff learn together and both those observed and those observing develop and deepen their understanding of how to improve learning. As importantly, the process creates descriptive evidence that can generate effective change across a school or authority. (Thomson, 2011: 6)

This approach has much to offer. It enables professionals to observe and reflect upon practice. It allows practice to be analysed and discussed in an objective non-judgemental way. It uses a fact-based approach which tries to get away from a fixed or imposed agenda. It is about reflecting upon the teaching rather than on the teacher, therefore it should reassure staff who don't want to be put under the spotlight and then be criticized for their actions.

As part of their toolkit, the team will suggest some reasons why staff should be involved:

- It makes a difference.

'Learning rounds can deliver high quality, sustainable improvements in the learning experiences of pupils in a range of contexts. It helps develop collegial practice and a positive ethos. Above all it is a motivating experience for participants.'

- It builds learning communities.

'Learning rounds offer teams, schools, clusters and authorities a straightforward and effective way to build a learning community, owned and led by teachers, focussed on what matters.'

- It supports continuous professional development (CPD).

'Learning rounds provides high quality CPD at 3 levels:

1. It promotes **individual learning** for each member of the **observation** team by building up understanding of what is effective learning and teaching.

2. It develops **the capacity of a school** and **authority** to create a culture of collegiality and shared learning in order to improve the learning experience of pupils.

3. It creates new capacity **to bring about system wide improvement**'.

(Thompson, 2011: 6, emphasis added)

The thrust of this approach is that it is the observers themselves who learn. Observation is not there to judge the practitioner, but to inform the observers on their 'rounds'. 'The group discussions which follow, create deeper understanding around the process of learning and teaching, especially on the learning experiences of pupils, and the process of effective change leadership' (Thompson, 2011: 6).

So learning rounds approach reflection as a collaborative process. This is a socio-constructivist approach where the group of voices produce more analysis than could be discovered by any single person. The observations are objective. There is no personal feedback – instead, there are conclusions drawn, based upon the observational evidence: 'there is no evaluation of the individual and the practice observed is described in non-evaluative language. There is no individual feedback' (Thompson, 2011: 6).

What do teachers think of learning rounds?

In terms of reflective practice, learning rounds do provide a clear structure. Putting aside the actual experience of having a group of fellow professionals observe you during your lesson, there is much benefit for those observing. They can witness practice, they can reflect on different ways of doing things and they have the opportunity to articulate their findings with others in a professional and constructive manner. The fact that it is about moving from several different observations into making more general conclusions about learning means that it is not as sharply focused upon personal learning and reflection.

> I enjoyed watching and then discussing what we saw in terms of learning. I feel
> I got ideas and had to think hard about professional practice. However, I wasn't

too keen on being watched. Having no feedback left me wondering what the others were thinking, and even though I know from my own experience of observing that it isn't personal, there's still that niggling doubt that you might have gone down in someone's estimation! (Primary school teacher, 2010)

As a tool for developing and widening experience and skills, it has much to offer those observing. From the perspective of the teacher being observed, it can be quite daunting knowing that a group of observers will be there during the lesson and that they will not be providing any detailed feedback or giving you the opportunity to discuss what happened and why. Of course, that isn't the point for learning rounds, yet for many participants there will be the stress of having them followed by lack of feedback comments. Many can be left wondering what the group 'really thought'.

As a consequence, a lot of schools do adapt the approach and allow some brief feedback to participants. However, the kind of reflection discussed in this book is based on a model where the teacher would always be given the opportunity to reflect and articulate on what happened, and why it happened, and to draw from the experience lessons about themselves as professionals who are continuing on a developmental journey.

Clearly, there is a different agenda to the model of personal professional reflections advocated in this book. The learning rounds approach provides evaluations for the bigger picture. They can identify strengths and weaknesses in an institution. They can, in some cases, provide information about individual practice. However, they do not enable the individual to 'work it out for themselves'. It is not a personal approach; it is not meant to be; it is about looking at examples of practice and drawing general conclusions. The next steps are also likely to be general ones.

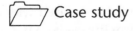 Case study

For example, a series of learning rounds in a primary school might identify a problem with the way the first 15 minutes are spent in the classroom each day. They might flag up the fact that, in their observations, there were many pupils engaged in too much admin and too little learning.

(Continued)

(Continued)

As a staff, there might be a decision to review the procedure for what happens in each class for those first 15 minutes. This might result in changes to some of the admin tasks that teachers were previously obliged to undertake.

Thus, the objective observations from the learning rounds team will have had an impact on the learning and teaching in every class in the school.

This is important and laudable for the whole school. However, this is quite different from the idea of a teacher and their personal, professional development, where they are encouraged to consider what it is they do with their class and how they might alter their own practice in order to improve things. This does not provide the space for personal reflection and problem solving for a problem that they identify and solve for themselves.

The difference here is that it was a whole-school change that was needed. In the professional articulation model, which will be outlined later in this book, it is the individual who can initiate change, who can reflect and see where change is needed. Yes, there will be ownership via the learning rounds, but there is still that niggling feeling that others are making judgements on the basis of a snapshot observation where you had little opportunity to 'speak for yourself'.

As part of a raft of measures, there is much to be gained from learning rounds, however it is a different kind of reflection that this book is searching for. It is worth also mentioning that learning rounds require several members of staff to be given time off-duty to be involved. In schools this means the need for supply cover or cover from the management team. Either way, it can be an expensive option for promoting professional reflection, and perhaps more affordable and sustainable approaches need to be considered.

Lesson study and reflective practice

Lesson study originates in the Far East, where it is practised widely in China and Japan. It is an approach to improving pedagogy and to understanding what works well, what does not, and why. 'In Japan the approach involved a small team of teachers working collaboratively over a three year period. In England the approach was modified so that the time frame was reduced to one half term' (Learning & Teaching Update, 2007).

In a lesson study process, groups of teachers identify an aspect of practice that is giving them grounds for concern, or that they are interested in developing. Together, they share their current understanding and the pedagogy they are familiar with. They then enquire into developments in teaching that are likely to have an impact on this aspect of pupil learning. They look at current literature and research to ascertain what current thinking is on the subject. Having brought their understanding up to date, the group then go on to plan a lesson which allows them to experiment and explore different approaches. Next, one member will teach the lesson whilst the others observe.

> The lesson is planned with the specific learning of three (or multiples of three – six or nine) pupils in mind. They are typical of different learner groups in the class (say lower, middle or higher attaining in that subject/aspect). Each stage of the lesson is planned with the needs of each of the three in mind and the lesson plan usually becomes the template upon which observations are noted during the research lesson – again in relation to the three case pupils.

> One teacher teaches and the others observe – always focusing on the behaviour and learning of the case pupils – what they were predicted to do and learn compared with what actually happened. (Learning & Teaching Update, 2007)

After the lesson, the group get together and review the lesson and the learning. They focus on the case study pupils and what their experience has been. The onus is on the development of the lesson, not on the individual teacher's practice. (There are obvious similarities with learning rounds in this respect.)

The lesson might then be modified in the light of the observations before another member of the group teaches it to their own class. At this point, the other group members observe, again keeping a focus on the specific learning of three pupils (as above).

The result is that the changes to the plan can be seen in action and, ideally, improvements witnessed. If successful, the plan is shared beyond the group – with the rest of the school, group of schools or beyond.

This collaboration enables professionals to reflect on practice. They feel ownership and feel free to experiment in a supported situation. The experience is focused and localized. Staff do not feel personally judged, but instead they feel part of a research experience designed to enable them to improve their own practice and to learn from each other and from current research and reading.

In addition, Japanese lesson study groups publish their findings.

> A lesson study group will focus on improving the teaching and pedagogic knowledge of how to teach a particular aspect of a subject through the processes of:
>
> • group analysis of need (pupil learning)
>
> • analysis of where the pedagogic knowledge gaps are in their practice (based upon evaluations of pupil performance), and
>
> • what recent research has to say about developments in this area.
>
> Evidence from Japanese and US research indicates that this focus on the case pupils helps to focus attention on learning and to deflect attention from the teacher, enabling a freer discussion to occur between members of the group. More open observations can be made, more potential solutions can be offered and more risks taken in discussion and reflections. This is because all members of the lesson study group own the lesson.
>
> Furthermore, the debate is not about the teacher – it is about the learning (or lack of it) for which they are all responsible. In addition, what did not work in the research lesson is as important to discover as what did (especially if it was something everyone at the outset assumed would work). (Learning & Teaching Update, 2007)

A strength of this approach is that the collaborative nature of the process means that reflection is very focused and participants are more willing to be creative and to take risks in experimenting with their practice and pedagogy.

Both school leaders and teachers in schools involved in the study strongly believed that the lesson study process encouraged risk-taking and a culture of professional learning both from what does not work as well as what does. Participants valued the fact that a research lesson is jointly owned by participants and felt this increased the likelihood of risk-taking and learning.

Teachers in their first three years of teaching found that engagement in the process gave them an opportunity to engage in 'deep' professional learning, not offered by existing models such as the standard diet of the induction year. It was used enthusiastically by participants in the Graduate Teaching Programme whose managers felt it provided valuable structured opportunities to learn from more experienced colleagues while actively engaging with them in joint teaching, observation and analysis.

Members of the pilot were clear that the distinctive elements of lesson study are: 'increased risk-taking [which] is enabled, through sharing the ownership of the lesson and its outcomes – which con-trasts sharply with much of the effects of inspection and perfor-mance management oriented observation which can lead teachers to play safe' (Learning & Teaching Update, 2007).

This approach has many benefits and interesting features. Certainly it would be very useful for mentoring and supporting staff new to the school or establishment. However, the focus is very much on the les-son, the specific planned practice, rather than on the reflection by the professional. Later in this book, I will suggest ways in which the les-son study and the learning rounds might fit into a raft of measures which build upon and support a more personal professional reflective process.

A coaching model

The notion of peer support has gained a lot of credibility in recent times. The idea that having someone to work with who was not an authority figure, who was not an expert, but instead someone at a similar stage of development is an attempt to get away from the inhibitions brought about by having 'judgement' getting in the way of authentic reflection. Teachers or students work together, coaching each other. They create their own agenda and pattern of working.

Again, observation generally features in the interaction. This is followed by discussion and reflection. This approach gets away from the fear that there is an externally imposed agenda. It avoids the stress of being made accountable and the feeling that judge-ments are being made. This approach does indeed free the players to focus more fully on their performance and its development. The constructivist approach to learning – now so prevalent in our schools – is manifested here in a peer-learning situation. The dia-logue between the players, the process, the fact that they are both learning at the same time, all of these are positives.

However, one concern might be that the very term 'coaching' conjures up images of one fit and competent athlete gently supporting and developing the skill and fitness of his protégé. The term 'coach' implies one person as expert. It might be intimidating to feel that the other person always knows more than you when you want to be developing jointly in a peer partnership. If you are the more able partner, you might feel that you are giving more than you are receiving if the roles defined are based upon the coach and the coached.

On the other hand, can we ever truly be peers in the sense that we are at the same stage in learning? Will there not still be that feeling of not wanting the other person to see our foolish mistakes? Will there not still be the sense that through compromise you end up avoiding or not getting the reflection and development you need? In a peer coaching dialogue, it is still too easy to have an imbalance, too easy to be dominated by the needs of the 'coach'.

My investigations into this approach left me feeling that, whilst having many advantages over the more traditional methods, it still had huge flaws that got in the way of authentic personal professional reflection.

Professional Monologues

What was needed, I felt, was an opportunity for a professional monologue. That is to say, a situation where one person can articulate their reflections, out loud to a sympathetic, non-judgemental audience, as if they were talking to themselves. It would be a monologue in the sense that it does not need the other person to comment, advise or problem-solve. No empathetic anecdotes or comparing of experiences would be required. The focus would be on one person reflecting and articulating while the other asked questions when required in order to enable the person reflecting to 'work things out for themselves'.

A Counselling Approach

The notion of a professional monologue would afford the professional with an opportunity to articulate reflection to an audience that would be non-judgemental, an audience without an agenda. This monologue would be an opportunity to reflect, without fear of interruption or contradiction. Such a monologue would enable the professional to reflect openly and honestly on the things that they felt were important and that they needed to talk about.

Such an approach would need certain conditions in order to succeed. It would need to be free from the sense of judgement. It would need to be 'owned' by the person reflecting. And it would need to be an opportunity to think about, reflect on and articulate their thoughts and feelings to an empathetic listener. The emphasis is on monologue and on an empathetic listener, and these skills will be discussed later in this book.

Of course, the first reaction to this suggestion may well be that there is still too much reliance on 'relationship', and on trust. This would be true. As you will read later on in this book, trust and feeling comfortable with the Peer Learning Partner are vital to the success of this approach. However, once established, the trust would not be about 'performance' but about enabling someone else to develop their practice. As Burbules and Rice posit, what is required is:

> tolerance, patience, respect for differences, a willingness to listen, the inclination to admit that one may be mistaken, the ability to reinterpret or translate one's own concerns in a way that makes them comprehensible to others, the self imposition of restraint in order that others may 'have a turn' to speak, and the disposition to express one's self honestly and sincerely. (Burbules and Rice, 1991: 441)

Other Considerations

Despite all that is written about professional reflection, there will always be a need for advice and guidance to be given and a need to monitor and improve standards and performance. From a personal, professional and management perspective, these improvements are an essential aspect of practice. Later in this book, we will look at the 'balancing act' where we try to provide 'space for the monologue', whilst at the same time being able to provide support and help when it is needed. The focus, however, for the reflective practice discussed will be on personalized professional development which is self-initiated, personally motivated and personally meaningful, and such that it also fulfils the demands and needs of the profession.

Later chapters will discuss how we might deliver the training to encourage 'reflective' cohorts in the workplace and some of the necessary skills required. We will look at how we might begin to separate accountability agendas from personal reflection and self-initiated development agendas.

Summary

This chapter has explored in some detail many of the different approaches to professional reflection. The development from authority-imposed reflection and judgement to more supportive collaborative reflection has been traced. A list of different initiatives have been presented and analysed with strengths and weaknesses identified. Finally, a suggestion that more of a 'counselling' model might afford more trust, independence and opportunity for authentic reflection free from authority agendas was introduced. This will be developed further later in this book.

 Questions for Reflection

Reflective questions to consider and discuss with a peer, who has the task of 'enabling' you to hold a professional monologue about this learning.

- What did you learn about the different ways of encouraging reflection?
- Were there any surprises?
- Consider your own experiences of reflection so far. Have you experienced any of those presented in this chapter? If so, which were useful and why? Which didn't work for you, and why not?
- Did you disagree with any of the comments in the chapter?
- Consider your first reaction to the notion of professional monologues to articulate learning.
- What would be the strengths? What would be the challenges?

Further Reading 📖

- Forde, C. and O'Brien, J. (2011) 'Policy and practice in education', No. 29. *Coaching and Mentoring: Developing Teachers and Leaders*. Edinburgh: Dunedin Academic Press, Chapters 2 and 3.
- Moon, J. A. (1999) *Reflection in Learning and Professional Development*. Abingdon: RoutledgeFalmer, Chapter 3.
- Reed, M. and Canning, N. (2010) *Reflective Practice in the Early Years*. London: Sage, pp. 7–23.
- Topping, K. (1996) *Effective Peer Tutoring in Further and Higher Education*, SEDA Paper 95. Available at: www.londonmet.ac.uk/deliberations/seda-publications/topping.cfm

References

Annett, N. (1997) *Collaboration and the Peer Tutor: Characteristics, Constraints, and Ethical Considerations in the Writing Center.* Available at: http://writing2.richmond.edu/training/fall97/nanne/peer.html

Boud, D., Cohen, R. and Sampson, J. (1999) 'Peer learning and assessment', *Assessment and Evaluation in Higher Education*, 24(4): 413–26.

Burbules, N.C. and Rice, S. (1991) 'Dialogue across differences: continuing the conversation', *Harvard Educational Review*, 61: 264–271.

Calderwood, J. and Shorrock, S. (1997), *Understanding Teacher Education: Case Studies in the Professional Development of Beginning Teachers.* London: Falmer Press.

Edwards, A., Gilroy, P. and Hartley, D. (2002) *Rethinking Teacher Education: Collaborative Responses to Uncertainty.* London: RoutledgeFalmer.

Forde, C. and O'Brien, J. (eds) (2012) *Coaching and Mentoring: Policy and Practice.* Edinburgh: Dunedin Academic Press.

Learning & Teaching Update website (2007) www.teachingexpertise.com/articles/the-lesson-study-model-of-classroom-enquiry-2950

Stevens, D. and Lowing, K. (2008) 'Observer, observed and observations: initial teacher education. English tutors' feedback on lessons taught by student teachers of English', *English in Education*, 42(2): 162–98.

Thomson, G. (2011) *Learning Rounds Toolkit.* Scottish Centre for Studies in School Administration. Available at: http://ltsblogs.org.uk/cpdteam/2011/02/09/learning-rounds-the-story-grows/

3

How can we make reflective practice more effective?

Chapter Overview

In this chapter, we will be looking at how we might enable these reflections to be articulated so that they can properly be considered, valued and thereafter have an impact on practice. The chapter examines:

- A constructivist approach
- Problems with terminology
- Peer tutoring
- Peer learning
- Professional articulations
- Advantages of the professional monologue
- Comments from teachers about reflection
- Professional monologues: a person-centred approach
- Setting the agenda
- Loaded questions
- An alternative vision
- Variation

In the last chapter, we looked at the many different forms of reflection that are associated with teaching and teacher training. Many of the traditional approaches have the added challenge in that they can be perceived, by the participants, as being about accountability and the promotion of agendas that belong to other people. It seems clear that in order for reflection to be effective, it needs to be, at least to some degree, self-initiated, and to have an accompanying sense of ownership for the person doing the reflection. This approach suggests that getting away from the sense of 'authority' would enable the person reflecting to be more open and honest and more able to seek change and more significant growth in their own learning. Actions and changes to practice are more likely to be tried; and experimenting and taking risks with new approaches are more likely, if there isn't the fear of being judged or criticized.

> Power relationships between staff and learners can inhibit reflection...a learner may skew their reflective activity to fit what they imagine is expected of them. (Moon, 1999: 170)

However, self-initiated reflection is only one element to be considered:

> Peer learning activities have an advantage over other teaching and learning strategies in that they have considerable potential to promote critical reflection. Critical reflection can focus on the topics being considered, the assessment activities themselves and the peer learning processes in which participants are engaged. They can do this if sufficient attention is given to the creation of a climate for learning and assessment which encourages reciprocal communication and openness to feedback. (Boud, 1997: 11)

It is not enough to merely look back upon practice and think about 'how to make it better'; it is also important to articulate the reflection if it is going to have any real impact upon practice.

A Constructivist Approach

So far in this book, we have focused upon this idea of reflection being most potent when it is genuine and self-initiated. However, such reflection is often buried in the day-to-day melee of practice. It is essential to stop, take stock and reflect with some sense of audience and purpose. The whole premise of modern learning theories is based upon Vygotsky's (1986) idea of constructing understanding. This idea of learning as being a social experience, where it is the interactions between the players that promote deep learning, is linked to the theory of scaffolding and the Zone of Proximal Development. These theories are well known to teachers when considering the learning of pupils in their care (Vygotsky, 1986).

What is needed now is for the same principles to be applied to the development of their own reflective skills. By encouraging teachers and students to work in pairs, teaming up to develop supportive 'learning conversations', we are creating a safe professional environment where true reflection can take place. Having the opportunity to reflect with an audience that you trust – who will not interrupt you, sidetrack you or judge you, and who will support you in taking these reflections forward into action – will add a new depth and a new dimension to personal, professional, reflective practice. Indeed, it can be argued that 'real' reflective practice needs another person as mentor or professional supervisor, who can ask appropriate questions to ensure that the reflection goes somewhere, and does not get bogged down in self-justification, self-indulgence or self-pity!

Ghaye and Ghaye suggest that: 'Reflections should be articulated in order to move from tacit and unconscious knowing, to more conscious knowing' (1998: 19–20). It is this consciousness that enables reflection to become the catalyst for change. Yet it is the articulation of the reflection that makes it much more tangible and enables one to be much more aware of it.

Problems with Terminology

Conversations – monologues … what's in a name?

The term we have used is not, in fact, *learning conversations*, but professional monologues. At first sight, this might seem to be a contradiction. The idea, despite arguing for reflection to be a shared construction of understanding, and something to be done with a supportive partner, seems to suggest that the 'learning conversation' should be just that. However, a conversation implies something quite different. This is more than a problem of semantics. The quality of reflection proposed in this book relies on quite a different understanding of 'what it is'. It would be wrong to use terms like learning conversations or professional consultations or coaching dialogues.

The crux of this approach is that the 'learner' needs to get there by themselves. The 'supporter' or facilitator is there to enable them to do so.

The problem with all of these other terms is that they imply a different kind of interaction.

What to call it?

For example, a 'learning conversation' sounds good in principle. It suggests two or more people having a conversation about their learning. The problem with this, however, is that the word 'conversation' implies that participants take turns in expressing thoughts, feelings and ideas. The players take their turns and each contributes what they can. This is not the approach being advocated here. Such an approach may lead to a focus on providing solutions, looking for a quick fix to a seemingly important problem. It often takes the form of one more dominant partner 'leading' the conversation and the conclusions. Such an approach can have too much of a focus on solving a problem and not enough focus on learning and meta cognition. It can still get in the way of personal, professional reflection where the person reflecting comes to their own conclusions and initiates change for themselves, and by themselves.

There is also the potential for going off the topic and instead exchanging personal anecdotes about similar experiences had by each of the participants. This is not to say that there should not be any joint construction of understanding. However, what is proposed here is that the interaction has different phases, the first phase being the facilitating of reflection, developing the articulation of analysis of practice and of understanding. After that might come the joint endeavour which involves a more collaborative, socially constructed look at practice, and develops approaches towards professional development and improvement of practice. (We will return to this in more detail later.)

'Professional consultations' gets a little nearer to the heart of the approach, however there is still a hint of the 'consultant' or 'expert' about the title. If the reflection is to be authentic and true, it needs to be the result of some 'discovery learning' with minimum input from others. Having a consultant or 'more knowledgeable other' can hinder the act of self-realization.

Kenneth Brufee (1987: 42–7) suggests that 'a peer is a person who has equal standing with another, such as in rank, class, or age, and he emphasizes that a peer is an equal, not a superior'.

A 'coaching partner' has the same problem. The notion of a coach is the same as that of an expert or 'more knowledgeable other', informing and influencing the inexperienced one to learn and develop. When we think of a coach, we imagine someone who knows many of the answers, someone who will show us the way and 'fix it for us'. Instead, we argue for self-help, a reflection that enables us to work it out for ourselves.

Peer Tutoring

Another approach we should consider is 'peer tutoring' Here we have two participants who are at a similar point in their learning. The socio-constructivist approach, where the two contribute to a joint construction of knowledge and understanding, underpins this initiative. Peer tutoring is summarized by Topping (1996) who explains: 'Peer tutoring is characterised by specific role taking: at any point someone has the job of tutor while the other(s) are in role as tutee(s).' Gillam (undated) reminds us that 'the words peer and tutor ought to be a contradiction in terms'. If one person is doing the tutoring, then, by implication, the other cannot be a peer in learning. So the peer learning approach works in situations where there can be a flexible shifting of roles that are understood and accepted by both parties. Moust and Schmidt (1992) found that students felt peer tutors were better than staff tutors at understanding their problems, that they were more interested in their lives and personalities, and were less authoritarian and less focused on assessment.

There are many advantages to the peer tutoring approach. Certainly, this has taken off in a big way in the primary school classroom and in Higher Education. The notion of peers each supporting the other in their learning has much to offer. Topping (1996) again goes on to suggest: 'The act of tutoring itself involves further cognitive challenge, particularly with respect to simplification, clarification and exemplification.' However, in terms of the reflective practice and professional articulations advocated in this book, the approach does fall short in one or two areas. The peer tutor approach needs one person to be in the controlling role; the temporary expert or leader. Meanwhile, the other participant is left as the subservient partner, the co-learner. Certainly, the roles are interchangeable and ever shifting as the two grapple with developing their understanding. However, it is much more difficult in these situations to have a particular focus on one person's experience, one person's learning and the journey of discovery as they articulate their reflections and realize things about their own professional practice. Having the tutee role will get in the way of having such a focus. Being the tutee leaves less opportunity or licence to dwell on the reflective elements of the interaction.

Person (1999: 69–86) puts the peer tutoring approach very simply:

'Teacher asks the student a question

Student answers the question

Teacher gives feedback on the answer

Teacher and student collaborate to improve the answer

Teacher assesses students' understanding of the question and answer.'

Yet for effective professional reflection, it is important for the person reflecting to try to 'work it out for themselves' rather than have their peers collaborate to 'improve them'. We remember best that which we discover for ourselves. It is easier to take advice we have arrived at ourselves. Therefore, a different approach is required.

Peer Learning

This title comes much closer to a definition of the approach this book is advocating. Peer learning suggests that:

- learning takes place by both participants
- the participants have equal status
- they have equal power
- the interaction is about the learning.

Peer learning interactions are about peers learning. Peer learning does what it says on the packet, with no nuances of power, agendas (overt or hidden) or instruction. Ideally, one might add something about the interaction being more of a professional articulation than a conversation, but that would make the title rather long!

It is important to stress that the learning is a peer learning opportunity. The person facilitating the professional articulations will learn much. They will learn about how another professional deals with day-to-day practice. They will hear about how peers tackle similar problems and opportunities. They will listen in on 'think alouds' as the other person works out what went well, and why. They will discover things about themselves as professionals and about the nature of their practice. They will also learn about active listening and how to enable others to reflect on and articulate their feelings and ideas. A life skill in itself, it is also an important element of many professions, from nursing to teaching, from social work to policing.

Some comments from peer learning interactions from student teachers:

He made me feel important.

It was quite nice that I had time to talk and figure out.

My supporter didn't just ask a question for the sake of it.

He was genuinely interested in what I had to say.

They listened to me, really listened and that doesn't happen everywhere.

They stayed quiet long enough to let me expand on it.

They gave me reassuring nods and relaxed me.

When I was thinking I didn't just get eyeballed, like, 'hurry up!'

There was no pressure.

She was really relaxed and neutral, not overly eager.

She was patient and made me comfortable, made me think about teaching.

Helped me to think about progression in a lesson.

Helped me to see the mastered skill of the pursed lip.

She had such a good way of wording her questions, made me think.

She was very friendly.

She made me think about how to apply things to other lessons.

She didn't just tell me, she made me think.

Professional Articulations

A 'professional monologue' comes close to the accurate definition of the approach. The person reflecting holds a monologue: that is, *a conversation with themselves*, in order to analyse what they can learn about themselves as a learner, a teacher/professional and a person.

It is a professional monologue because it has its focus on professional learning: learning that is not inhibited by fear of judgement, accountability or a focus on somebody else's agenda.

Whereas the other terms allow opportunity for personal anecdote and interpersonal irrelevancies, this approach tries to maintain a focus on the reflections in a professional manner. This is the role of the peer, the learning facilitator – they need to develop skills that are more akin to counselling than to being a coach, mentor or expert. 'Through communication, exploration, challenge and justification ... shifts in perspective, attitude and values can arise' (Ghaye and Ghaye, 1998: 19–23).

Advantages of the Professional Monologue

It is probably a truism to say that all professionals reflect upon their practice. There will be many times a day, per hour, or in a lesson when reflection goes on. The problem is that it goes on only *inside* the head. This may or may not lead to some sort of action or change. Reflecting on the disaster of today's experience provides a huge amount of impetus to strive to make tomorrow better. However, this 'firefighting' approach does not provide lasting change. This kind of response to the day-to-day happenings is not what is meant here by professional reflection. There needs to be some sense of perspective, a sense of having the opportunity to stop, think about, reflect on and articulate those reflections.

Comments from Teachers about Reflection

When interviewed about reflection, some experienced teachers reported: 'Yes, we reflect all the time, but we don't get to discuss it with anyone.' When asked why this was, this is what they said:

> Nobody is really that interested. If you go into the staffroom and say how difficult the morning has been, you are more likely to have colleagues responding with how much more difficult their morning has been. It's more like one-upmanship sometimes. Or, even if not, even if there is sympathy, that's all it is, it's much more personal than professional. I still leave the staffroom feeling no further forward as a teacher. (Teresa, class teacher, primary school)

When I asked why professional dialogue didn't take place more often, I was told that there was simply no time. Clearly, staff are too pressured about the 'nitty-gritty' of their task to feel able to focus on reflecting professionally, and certainly the opportunities for this to happen successfully in an incidental way are limited. (As you will see in Chapter 6 with the case studies, the approach promoted in this book seems to have helped on both of these counts.)

One of the things staff who took part in peer learning interactions appreciated about the professional monologue was the ability to sit and talk and not have to worry about whether or not their colleague was interested, or that they were about to interrupt with their own 'stuff'. The opportunity to think and talk things through is one of the benefits of this approach. The fact that it is with a trusted 'other', who is not there to judge them, or to try to supply a 'quick fix', is another benefit. Post Graduate Diploma students explained it like this:

> I think it would be a good thing to promote because, at the schools I've been in, at break there's a lot of teachers sounding off anyway, but it's all about the children, about what they've done, but it's not professional, not about the teacher and what they do and could do to make things better. If you give people opportunities to reflect on their practice then it might have some effect on what they do.

> It's good not having somebody talking while you reflect because, if you're having a conversation, sometimes when somebody's speaking, you might be thinking of what you're going to say next. There's not much space to go into the depth, and I think that having that time to really stop and think – get the cogs of the brain turning around – it helps you to realise what you've done. Sometimes it took quite a long time. And the structure gives a slight formality to it doesn't it? It takes it away from being a casual chat. (Sue and Kelly, PGDE students)

Professional Monologues: A Person-centred Approach

This idea of enabling professional monologues uses a counselling approach to provide a framework and structure, so that one person can facilitate for their peer to develop their understanding through professional articulations. In this way, we have a mirror of the person-centred counselling model, where one person adopts the role of facilitator whilst the other articulates their own developing understanding. The person-centred approach is based on the work of the American Carl Rogers (1957). It is sometimes referred to as 'client-centred counselling', 'non-directive counselling' and sometimes just as 'counselling'. It is this idea of 'non-directive' interaction that is at the heart of peer learning interactions.

Cooper (2008: 120) describes a person-centred approach where 'the counsellor aims to create a particular kind of relationship with his or her clients within which the client is enabled to discover his or her own resources for moving towards a more satisfying way of being'. He goes on to explain the conditions for such an interaction: 'The counsellor attempts to offer a relationship which, by its quality of respect, understanding and openness, makes possible for the client a new appraisal of self and an opportunity for change and development' (p.120). He suggests that this approach is consistent with initiatives from The Scottish Executive who present a definition of counselling for support in schools as 'A process whereby one person helps another using a style of listening which is non-judgmental, non-directive, of a reflective nature, and which encourages clients to work through their issues' (p.120).

Whilst the reader might react to the use of the word 'client', it is clear that this is a similar approach to that described in this book. The notion of a 'client' does not sit comfortably with the concept of peer reflection and learning. It goes back to the idea of a 'less experienced' or 'novice' who learns from an 'expert'. However, the description of the kind of relationship here is an accurate portrayal of peer learning interactions, as is the philosophy of the style of listening and supporting discussed throughout this book.

This is where a more socio-constructivist approach comes in. The interaction begins with one person enabling the other to 'stop, think, reflect, articulate', but then the two work together to construct a shared understanding. Together, they explore what happened, why it happened, how this might influence them as professionals, and how it might inform developments in their practice.

The word 'issues' used in the quote above from Cooper also smacks of someone with 'problems' to be addressed. It sounds like a deficit model of reflection. Whereas the point of professional reflection is that it both acknowledges good practice, and builds towards the development of improving practice, it does not see experience as 'bad', or practice as having 'issues', but instead sees practice as something to be constantly reflected upon in an objective way with a problem-solving approach to improvement.

In order to leave room for this dialogue and the potential for development, roles in the peer learning interaction are not fixed or restrictive. At some point, both participants move into a socio-constructivist relationship where they work together to develop their understanding and create ideas and strategies to improve and develop their practice: 'The reflective conversation is a medium through which we are able to learn from our teaching experiences and question the educational values that give it shape, form and purpose' (Ghaye and Ghaye, 1998: 16).

In summary, the whole process can be described as:

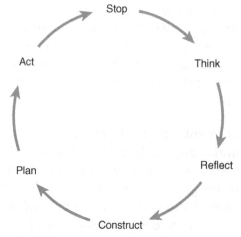

Figure 3.1   Cycle of reflection

Here we move from thinking to articulating, then from co-constructing understanding to planning developments in practice, finally arriving back in practice where we put all of these reflections and ideas into action. This will be explored in more detail elsewhere in this book.

A person-centred approach towards reflective practice

Rogers (1957) believed that we all have the potential for:

- sociability: the need to be with other human beings and a desire to know, and be known, by other people
- being trusting and trustworthy
- being curious about the world, and open to experience
- being creative and compassionate.

He described the 'core conditions' that are needed by a counsellor in order to bring about change. The main three conditions, described in *The Person Centred Approach to Counselling: A Short Introduction* (Rogers, 2012) are:

1. **Empathy** – Rogers said that if this condition is in place, the counsellor is 'experiencing an accurate, empathic understanding of the client's awareness of his own experience'. He stressed the importance of the counsellor showing this understanding to the client.

2. **Unconditional positive regard** – This means that the counsellor is accepting and absolutely non-judgemental of the client. Rogers

said the counsellor is acceptant of all the parts of the client; it is the opposite of saying 'you are bad in these ways, good in those'. It is completely unconditional in that there is no element of 'I only like you if you are thus and so'.

3. **Congruence** – Rogers said this means that the counsellor, in the confines of the therapeutic relationship, is a 'congruent, genuine and integrated person'. He said it means that the counsellor does not either intentionally or unintentionally hide behind a façade or front; that he or she actually is the person they are feeling themselves to be at the time.

Let us consider these core conditions in terms of professional reflection.

Empathy: This is essential if the participants in the reflective process are going to be able to feel relaxed and in an environment of trust. Getting away from a fixed agenda and from a sense of being judged might be one way of creating an environment for the kind of empathy where there is the freedom to reflect honestly. Having a peer who is at the same stage of development as you might also enable more of a climate where empathy is possible. Knowing the other person personally as well as professionally might also be beneficial.

Unconditional positive regard: This is something to strive for. With the best will in the world, it is difficult when talking about oneself not to feel judged in some way. The peer learning interactions described suggest that there should be a climate of non-judgement. The setting up of the interaction should provide the potential for a developing relationship where participants feel safe and more independent of the kind of power relationship that might inhibit true reflection. Later in the book, we will look at different kinds of interaction. It might be that discussing practice that has *not* been observed by your peer, provides more freedom and greater empathy than those instances that they have witnessed.

Congruence: There is more possibility of a congruent relationship when there is no assessment, no judgement and no agenda fixed by an external agency. Here the peer learning interaction has many benefits over the alternatives. Two peers, at the same point in their learning, working together to professionally reflect on their practice in a non-judgemental environment provide many of the ingredients for a congruent relationship.

Skills

Of course, such an approach requires a certain level of skill for both parties. If you are going to be the one who facilitates, encourages, guides without interfering, without advising, without judging yourself, you need to have some kind of training.

There needs to be an agreed protocol, with a set structure as a framework or guide to the interaction, and there needs to be a shared understanding of the process and its aim. There will need to be an agreement of ownership. There should be an understanding that the discussion or monologue is confidential, or as confidential as the reflector wishes it to be.

Trust

Certainly, there will need to be a degree of trust. When trialling peer learning interactions set up for students in ITE, it was the students themselves who established the partnerships and made arrangements for meeting up to explore their professional reflections together, the premise being that they would feel more comfortable with someone with whom there was already a degree of trust. Where this was not possible, due to the geography of the placements, students still managed interactions with someone they did not know. In the survey (see Chapter 6), it was surprising to find that the students who did not already know their partners did not in fact feel that there was any problem in terms of trust. However, those who had self-selected their peer learning partner did, in fact, list 'working with someone that I know and trust' as being beneficial to the success of the interaction. The conclusion would seem to be that, yes, it is ideal to work with someone that you know and trust and feel is truly a 'peer', as opposed to someone who you feel has authority over you. But if this is not possible, and you do not know your partner well, it doesn't mean that the professional interaction will flounder. Indeed, the structure, question bank and ethos of the approach are there to ensure that the session is professional and not personal. (More details of this will be explored in the next chapter.)

There may be a fear that using a counselling approach might trigger something more personal in the interaction. Again, the way the peer learning interaction is structured should prevent this being an uncomfortable experience that is more personal than professional. However, it is important to acknowledge that there may be issues that arise, and consequently it is important that those involved establish the ethos and 'ground rules' of the interaction before proceeding. (The ethos of this whole approach and the structure regarding what is to be discussed and how it is discussed are covered in more detail in Chapter 4.)

Setting the Agenda

From the outset, we have argued that the person doing the reflecting should 'own' the agenda. If they are the one to decide what is articulated, they will feel much more secure and in control. If they can choose for themselves the focus for the session, then they will not perceive questions as being 'loaded' or having some hidden agenda driving them. The advantage of this is that the reflection is personal to them, there is an opportunity for the professional to reflect upon elements of practice at a time and in a way that they are ready to do. If the person reflecting initiates the focus for the interaction then they will feel more empowered, more in control and less threatened or judged.

Unlike 'learning rounds', which may look at practice in a non-personal, general and whole-institution way, or a 'tutor/mentor observation', which may look at practice in a judgemental, measuring-against-the-standard way, the peer learning interaction seeks to allow the person reflecting to provide a personal, professional focus on an area that they identify themselves. Such an area is one that they feel they need to investigate further in order to advance their own development.

For example, it may well be that there are all sorts of problems for a teacher with the management of behaviour in the class. An observer might focus on this as the most obvious area needing support and development. However, if the teacher concerned wants to put that aside for the time being and to focus on the pupil learning instead, then they should be permitted to do so. So much of reflection seems to focus on behaviour. Yes, this is an important element of teaching and learning, but if the reflector can choose to discuss something else some of the time, then they have the opportunity to develop their overall performance. If there is a problem with classroom behaviour, then there are other ways of supporting that. It may be that this is something that a session can be devoted to. However, so much better if the reflector comes to that decision themselves. It is worth considering here the idea that reflection might be enhanced if the person facilitating does not actually witness the lesson.

 Case study

'It's better for me that you did not observe my lesson. I feel a lot better talking about it because although I know that there was some irritating behaviour that went on, you didn't focus on it or make me talk about it. I got to leave that for now and talk more about the learning. You helped me to have a chance to think about the lesson and the learning for a change, and that can only help me with the class behaviour in the long run.' (Alan, 4th-year BEd student)

This approach, where we have the professional peer learning interaction without observation, has many advantages. Traditionally, the person with the advanced skill or in authority will observe the novice in action prior to a 'discussion' that comes afterwards. One of the problems with this approach is that the person who needs to reflect will interpret any questions and comments in terms of what they think the observer saw or in terms of what they are 'judging'.

Loaded Questions

For example, if there is a question such as:

'Tell me what happened when you gave out the paints at the start of the lesson.'

The person reflecting is likely to think:

'Oh no, what did happen? Was someone misbehaving and I missed something?'

It is impossible for any question to appear neutral if you are working to someone else's list of questions, or to their agenda, or if they have just observed you teaching.

It is because of this that an approach is advocated here where the peer supporter does not witness the lesson. By taking the observation out of the equation, you remove many of the elements that get in the way of genuine professional reflection. Consider the same question again.

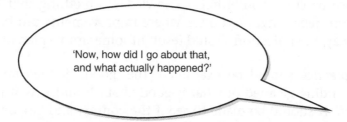

'Tell me what happened when you gave out the paints at the start of the lesson.'

This time the person reflecting is likely to think:

'Now, how did I go about that, and what actually happened?'

This approach enables the question to be more neutral. It allows and encourages reflection through description. Through the process of describing what happened, and reflecting and evaluating this in terms of the objective of the activity, there is much more potential for self-realization and honest self-evaluation to occur. The alternative might be that the question seems 'loaded', and the response might be to close down professional reflection and instead revert to being defensive and to look for excuses and explanations for 'practice not being perfect'.

> When I spoke to someone who had not seen me teach I had to describe and analyse in much greater detail what went on. I was not able to make any assumptions about the other person already knowing something.
>
> When I had a conversation with the person who had seen me teaching I left a lot out about my lesson because she had seen it for herself and therefore I felt it was irrelevant to our conversation.
>
> However in having a conversation with someone who did not see me teach I realised the significance of those things I had previously left out and how beneficial the discussion of them was to me and my partner. (Student, PGDE Primary)

Any approach that encourages reflection is valuable. Any approach where the person reflecting is obliged to describe their practice in an evaluative and analytical manner, is going to be useful in any profession. The approach puts them into a situation where they need to describe, in a concise professional manner, what they did and how it went. They are free from feeling threatened or judged, safe in the knowledge that they know what happened and the other person does not. They are supported in taking a step back and considering how effective their actions were. This freeing up enables them to articulate what they did, the reasons for their choices and the consequences of their actions. This provides a much deeper level of reflection than the traditional observation and feedback approach.

How can we enhance the effectiveness of reflective practice?

Of course, reflecting is only part of this process. It is important to do something with the reflections, or at least to use the reflection to influence practice. You either acknowledge something that is good and worth repeating, or you see where improvements can be made. Either way, the reflection should result in some simple plan of action.

Good practice should be examined, the 'good' defined and some understanding gleaned of what is good about it and why it is good. Some effort should be made to see if the context and circumstances can be replicated with the same positive result another time. Poor practice should also be examined. This would be a problem-solving exercise with the aim of identifying what happened, where it fell short of expectations, and how this might be approached differently another time with a successful outcome. This is where the person facilitating would shift their role and become more of a partner in exploring the reflections and ways of developing practice. This co-construction might result in some kind of action plan to develop understanding and have an impact upon further practice. We will look at ways of recording these plans in more detail in Chapter 8.

An Alternative Vision

The 'alternative vision', then, is for staff to have regular peer learning interactions. One person will be the enabler who asks the lead questions focusing on one particular aspect of practice. The person reflecting will try to describe and articulate what happened and how it happened, and then draw conclusions about their own practice. From this, the two people involved will arrive at a plan designed to maintain the good elements and add to this any improvements on the 'not so good'. Practice is thus developed and the professional has a heightened awareness of their practice and how it is developing. Moreover, the person enabling this encounter will also learn from their peer. Not only will they learn from the description of practice, but also about reflecting and working out how to maintain and improve the standard of that practice. (More details of the approach and how practitioners view its benefits are discussed in more detail elsewhere in this book.)

Variation

Of course, for reflection to be beneficial it has to be done frequently. The whole idea of continuous professional development is that we have an ongoing dialogue about our practice. What is advocated in this book is that practitioners have opportunities to reflect and to articulate their reflections so that they develop an understanding of their own abilities and professional 'needs'. However, if we always did the reflection in the same way, it would become routine, repetitious and boring. It is important to have a variety of approaches and within each one an opportunity to make adjustments in order to keep things fresh and to change the focus as and when required. (These variations are discussed in more detail later on in this book.)

Summary

In this chapter, we looked at the notion of professional reflection as a socially constructed practice. The idea of a reflective conversation was mooted, but with it came the challenge of defining exactly what was meant by conversation. Rather than a conversation, it was suggested that a professional monologue was facilitated in a peer learning interaction. Although coaching, tutoring and peer learning were all explored, it was more of a 'person-centred' counselling approach that was advocated. Such an approach might enable a professional exploration of practice, free from any sense of interrogation, judgement or accountability agendas. Factors such as trust, appropriate skills and variation in the approach were considered. Case studies from students

(Continued)

(Continued)

and teachers were used to illustrate some of the challenges and obstacles that prevent teachers from engaging more consistently in professional reflection. An alternative approach towards reflection was suggested. The suggestion of some benefit being gained from professional articulations to a peer were explored, and consideration was given to whether it was always essential to witness someone during their practice in order to facilitate their reflections about it. Finally, the idea was raised that reflection could become stale and tedious if we all did the same thing in the same way when we reflect, consequently there is the need for a varied approach.

Questions for Reflection

- Consider the 'loaded questions' part of this chapter. Have you been in a situation where the question seemed loaded? Did it make you feel judged and defensive?
- Think about the difference between discussing your practice with someone who has seen you in action compared with discussing it with someone who has not.
- List the advantages and disadvantages of these two approaches.
- Consider the advantages and disadvantages of discussing practice in a reflective manner with a peer as opposed to discussing it with someone in authority.
- Consider the benefits to the person doing the enabling in a peer learning interaction – is there as much to be gained for them?

Further Reading

- Bolton, G. (2010) *Reflective Practice*, 3rd edn. London: Sage. pp. 3–15.
- Brookfield, S. D. (1995) *Becoming a Critically Reflective Teacher*. San Francisco, CA: Jossey-Bass, Chapter 7.
- Ghaye, A. and Ghaye, K. (1998) *Teaching and Learning through Critical Reflective Practice*. London: David Fulton, Chapter 2.

References

Brufee, K. (1997) in Annett, N. (1997) *Collaboration and the Peer Tutor: Characteristics, Constraints, and Ethical Considerations in the Writing Center.* http://writing2.richmond.edu/training/fall97/nanne/peer.html

Clark et al. (1999: 79) cited in McGhie, M. and Barr, I. (2001: 79) 'Learning and Ethos', *Turning the Perspective*, Enschede, The Netherlands: CIDREE / SLO: Consortium of Institutions for Development and Research in Education in Europe/ Netherlands Institute for Curriculum Development.

Cooper, M. (2008) *Counselling in Schools Project Phase II: Evaluation Report*. Glasgow: University of Strathclyde.

Gillam, A. M. (undated) 'Collaborative learning theory and peer tutoring practice', in J.A. Mullin and R. Wallace (eds) *Intersections: Theory–Practice in the Writing Centre*. City of Illinois: The National Council of Teachers of English. 53–65.

Ghaye, A. and Ghaye, K. (1998) *Teaching and Learning through Critical Reflective Practice*. London: David Fulton.

Moust, J. C. and Schmidt, H. G. (1992) Undergraduate Students as Tutors: Are They as Effective as Faculty in Conducting Small-group Tutorials? Paper presented at the American Educational Research Association Symposium on Rewarding Teaching at Research Universities, San Francisco, CA, 23 April.

Person, N. K. (1999) 'Evolution of discourse during cross age tutoring' in *Cognitive Perspectives on Peer Learning*. Mahwah, NJ: Lawrence Erlbaum, pp.69–85.

Rogers, C. (1957) 'The necessary and sufficient conditions for therapeutic personality change', *Journal of Consulting Psychology*, 21(2): 95–103.

Rogers, C. (2012) *The Person Centred Approach to Counselling: A Short Introduction*. Available at: www.personcentredapproachsw.org/bb/pc.php

Topping, K. (1996) *Effective Peer Tutoring in Further and Higher Education*, SEDA Paper 95. Available at:www.londonmet.ac.uk/deliberations/seda-publications/topping.cfm

Vygotsky, L. (1986) *Thought and Language*. Cambridge, MA: Harvard University Press. Originally published 1934.

4

The challenges, benefits and possible solutions to using reflection in a professional context

Although this chapter might appeal to readers with a management responsibility, it is not aimed simply at them. Individuals who are motivated to take responsibility for their own professional development might be interested in reading how they could introduce some form of articulated learning in their own situation. The approach is designed to work in any context where one person is competent and trusted to facilitate the professional articulations of another, therefore the chapter does not need to be seen as the sole province of management.

It is difficult to present a scheme for introducing the peer learning interactions approach without taking into account the context where it is to be introduced. Different settings will provide different challenges. Obviously, the way this is approached will vary depending upon who is introducing it, where it is to be implemented and when. If a manager or ITE tutor was introducing this idea, they would take quite a different approach to a teacher in a school who feels it is a good idea. However, whether this is delivered to a large group, staff team or only to another individual, there are still some features of the approach that need to be explored.

Getting Started: Key Features

There are five main steps to introducing the peer learning approach. These are listed below before a more detailed examination in the rest of this chapter.

---

1   Establish the need for and importance of reflection: exploring the motivation for reflection.
2   Explore the skills and aptitudes required.
3   Establish trust and the 'ground rules' for interaction.
4   Develop a structure to support the interaction.
5   Agree what kind of outcome and evidence are required from the interaction.

Motivation to Reflect

It is important for participants to see where reflective practice fits into the bigger picture and into the definition of professionalism. For emerging professionals, this might be the first introduction to meta-cognition and the concept of reflecting on practice before planning the next steps for development. For existing professionals, this might be more of a revision of something they know already, or indeed that they do already, albeit in a less structured way. Most professionals would say that they do reflect a lot of the time, especially 'in practice'. Observing, thinking through, reflecting and then adapting, are things which an experienced professional does many times a day, every day.

Van Manon (1991) proposes a categorization of reflection:

- thinking and acting in a common-sense manner
- focusing on events and incidents
- reflection on personal experience and that of others
- reflection on the manner of reflection.

The Need for Reflective Practice

In order for those involved to understand and feel a part of this process, it is important to establish how the process of reflection can be beneficial to one's professional reflection. It is important to believe that there is a point to it beyond any managerial agenda. Reflection should be something initiated by the individual, for the individual. This is one of the biggest challenges. Many professionals believe themselves too busy to waste time chatting about their day. They consider that being professional means that they have a commitment to 'get on and do a good job', and may feel that stopping to discuss what they do and how they do it is an intrusion to them getting on with it.

> Privacy of practice leads to isolation and isolation is the enemy of improvement. (Elmore, 2007)

In the Scottish context of the Standard for Initial Teacher Education, the emphasis is quite clear. Professionalism involves 'taking responsibility for, and being committed to, your own professional development arising from professional enquiry and reflection on your own *and other* professional practices' (The Scottish Government, 2001). In the English Professional Standard for Teachers, one of the professional attributes required is to 'reflect on and improve their practice, and take responsibility for identifying and meeting their developing professional needs' (DfE Teacher Standards, 2011). But perhaps more convincing is the argument from Tony Ghaye (2011):

> To be called a reflective conversation there needs to be some consideration and questioning of the educational values that the teacher is commited to and tries to live out in his or her work.... Our professional values are those fundamentally important things that make us the kind of teacher we are. They give our teaching its shape, form and purpose. Clarifying, justifying and trying to live these values out are things every teacher should strive to do. (Ghaye, 2011: 43)

This element of 'talking to confirm what we think we already know' is another strong argument for stopping to reflect. Many times in our professional life we might lose perspective and begin to doubt our own beliefs and values. A peer learning interaction may well enable that professional perspective to be clarified.

Being professional is about developing professional values and attitudes. Yet we rarely stop and reflect on what these are. It is all too easy to get caught up in the day-to-day routines and demands of practice, to stop and reflect on what we are doing, why we are doing it, and what impact it is having. As professionals, we need to be aware of how our practice is impacting on those we are *responsible for* as well as those we are *responsible to*. Sometimes the demands of those who make us accountable are much more pressing than the demands of those we are engaged to provide for. By stepping back from the demands of the practicalities of the job, we may be able to see more clearly how our practice reflects our professional values.

In some sense, many professionals do not know how much they need these opportunities to reflect until they experience them first hand. In Kolb's learning cycle, there is a clear link from experience to reflection and the development of practice. We can adapt this cycle to accommodate reflection and development using a peer learning approach, as shown below.

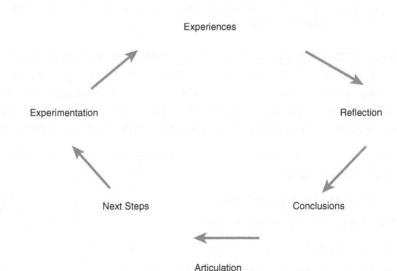

Figure 4.1   Adapted from Kolb's Learning Cycle

It is important that there is space to reflect and opportunity to articulate these reflections. However, it is also important that the next steps are considered and planned, and these might include ideas to explore and experiments to be created which might enhance future performance. Ghaye and Ghaye (1998: 4) express it thus: 'It is a view that we do not just receive and apply someone else's theory to our practice, but we hold and develop our own theories about practice.'

Introducing This Approach as a Leader

I have found that in many cases it is only when you demonstrate the process, by getting the participants to give it a try, that they realize that there is indeed some value in it for them. For example, one teacher told me:

> We discovered we had to actually go through the process and reach that conclusion for ourselves. In other words someone telling us about reflection and the positive outcomes wasn't enough, we had to do it for ourselves, become part of it and take ownership for it to have meaning and relevance. Also, in some way to remove the feeling that what we were doing was only because it was 'expected' either by management, parents, society, other demands etc. (Dianne, primary school teacher)

Another told me:

> It was so good to have the opportunity to stop and talk, knowing that there was someone who would listen and not judge, interrupt or sidetrack me. I can see how this might help me to get my head around what's been going on for me. (Morag, primary school teacher)

Working with a group, particularly if you have a captive audience and you are in a management role, you have more opportunity to encourage staff to listen to the reasons why this approach might be beneficial. You might use mind maps, carousels or other approaches which would encourage them to consider important questions like:

What is professionalism?

How do we develop as professionals?

What does professional reflection mean?

How do we reflect?

How do we structure and record our reflections?

How do we use our reflections to improve our practice?

However, it is still true that a workshop, lecture or research paper does not compare with encouraging someone to sit down, stop and try to articulate their reflections on their practice.

This does involve some skills on your part, however, and these skills are also an important aspect of what you will need to do to help them to develop, if you are going to have them become fully involved in the whole process.

Developing the Core Skills Required

Talking for listening, listening for learning

It is important to consider the different roles in the interaction. One way of doing this might be to consider the options. What kind of interactions might fit into this approach to talking about your reflections?

Facilitating

The person doing the facilitating will need some important interpersonal skills. They will need:

- good body language when in this counselling role

- good eye contact

- good listening skills (with an ability to actively listen and to 'piggy-back' on what the other person says and respond in a contingent way)

- to be able to ask open questions which enable the other person to reflect and analyse their own practice

- to be able to restate what they have heard

- to be able to reinterpret for the person reflecting so that they can see how their practice appears

- to be able to summarize and support in the setting of targets.

Reflecting

The person reflecting will also need to develop a range of skills. They will need:

- to be able to feel comfortable with the other person

- to be able to describe their practice in a thoughtful, reflective way

- to be able to articulate what they are thinking about

- to commit to the process and to trust the other person.

There are many ways to develop these skills, either on a personal level, as a pairing or small group, or as a whole establishment. One tried-and-tested approach is outlined below. This works well with professionals, students, and, as you will see in Chapter 7, even in a primary school!

Talking for listening

It is useful to think about interviewing here. Consider situations where you might have been interviewed. What did you enjoy? What wasn't so good? What did a good interviewer do to help you feel at ease to answer the questions as well as you could?

Next you might consider some famous examples of interviewers from television: Michael Parkinson, Jonathan Ross, Graham Norton or Chris Evans. You might look at what it is that makes some of these better than others at getting their guests to speak honestly and reflectively. What is it that they do that helps the guest to 'do the talking'?

Talking for learning

It is important that participants feel able to talk about their practice freely. There is a difference between 'chatting' about your day and articulating reflections about your professional practice. For those involved, this means considering the kind of questions that might help to unlock this professional dialogue. It means being able to analyse what happens in practice and come up with possible reasons for the success or lack of it that results from this practice. 'Making sense is not just a process of having a private conversation with yourself about your teaching, it also involves coming to know, through teacher talk and the sharing of experiences' (Ghaye and Ghaye, 1998: 6). It may be useful to begin with some reflections on 'safe' topics.

Discuss something you can remember learning, e.g. riding a bike; swimming; juggling; a foreign language; a maths formula; a set of facts; the spelling of a difficult word; origami; a yoga position.

Discuss why this is memorable – what is remembered?

What can we learn about these recollections?

Actively listening is much more difficult, though, than we think. It is so easy to think we are listening but in fact we are considering our own response or our next question.

> We discovered that we are not great at 'active listening'. During discussions we are learning slowly how to not impose our own viewpoints, without truly considering what someone else has to say. Several staff have commented (myself included) that it is difficult to really listen, because you instantly make a decision within the first piece of information from the speaker, and then your mind focuses on formulating your response, i.e. we have discovered we don't truly listen, but spend most time waiting for the moment to say what we think. (Dianne, primary school teacher)

This skill is one which needs careful consideration and practice. It may be some time before we 'get it right'. The most important thing is that we are asking open questions which get the other person talking professionally, and that we do little of the talking ourselves. Having a selection of questions ready is a good place to begin.

Question Banks

One good approach would be to work out a question bank which enables professional reflection to be articulated. In terms of teaching, this might involve questions such as:

Reflective Question Bank

- Talk me through what happened.

- Were there any surprises?

- What pleased you most?

- What was disappointing?

- What was the purpose of the lesson?

- What did the children learn today that they did not already know?

- What did you want the children to remember from this lesson? What do you think they will remember?

- Do you think the class learned what you wanted them to? How do you know? What will you do to support and develop this next time?

- How will you provide support for all learners? How will you know if this is successful?

- What kind of thinking did you encourage today? How do you know?

- Can you say the extent to which 'thinking about children as learners' influenced the approach that you adopted?

- Can you describe another lesson where content and purpose influenced you to use a different approach?

- What kind of feedback would you give yourself for this lesson?

- What did you learn about yourself today?

- What did you learn about teaching and learning today?

- What are your next steps to follow today's discussion?

(This question bank can also be found as an Appendix at the end of the book so that it is easier to photocopy.)

The questions are merely a starting point. It is not intended that they are worked through in some systematic way. Instead, they should provide a structure to ensure that the conversation is a 'reflective, professional discussion', rather than an anecdotal 'sounding off'. It is important to add to them, miss some of them out or substitute them with something more relevant if so doing enables a reflective conversation to take place.

For other professions, there would be a similar list, but with more emphasis on elements of that profession as opposed to questions about teaching. It may be that at certain times, for particular reasons, there will need to be additional 'focus questions' added to the bank in order to encourage the reflector to consider some elements of their practice in more detail. It is important to stress though that such a list must not be used as a cast-iron structure for the interaction. It would not be appropriate, nor very natural, to go through the list question by question. Such an approach would feel artificial and not conducive to genuine reflection.

Much more effective would be to internalize the question bank and select from it the questions to ask in order to get the session going.

Once the other person is talking about their professional practice, it is more important to listen actively and to 'piggy-back' on what they say. Such an approach enables the person articulating to feel at ease, to feel 'listened to' and frees them to think, talk and explore their reflections unrestricted by the confines of a question list.

Skills

Once you have considered supporting what to ask and what to say it is important to consider the skills required for success.

A learning interaction **needs:**

- positive, encouraging body language

- active listening

- open questions

- thinking time

- encouragement for professional reflection

- supportive feedback

- support in articulating understanding.

An effective Learning Interaction **does not need**:

- someone who dominates the conversation

- too many questions

- empathetic anecdotes

- judgemental reactions

- advice

- comparisons.

Developing these skills is an ongoing process, however having some time to spend on discussion and on establishing the questions and format is a worthwhile investment. Having a clear structure that is 'owned' by the participants is essential for the success of this approach.

Defining and establishing roles

Possible roles in an interaction

Coach and coached

Tutor and tutee

Expert and novice

Mentor and apprentice

Counsellor and counselled

Each of these has something to offer, but it is important to establish the kind of relationship that is going to best facilitate the kind of reflection discussed in this book. Coaching sounds like one person is the expert who has the role of coaching the other, so this needs to be explored. The whole principle of the peer learning approach is based upon the learning being self-learning and the emphasis should be on 'working it out for one's self'. Similarly, tutor and tutee implies a power relationship where one person will be able to tell the other what they should do.

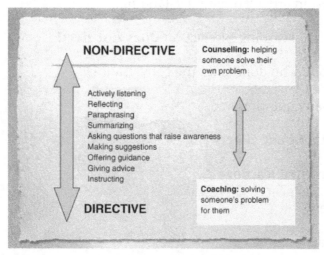

Figure 4.2   Progression of roles in learning interactions

Source: Tarrant (2008)

From the list of roles, the only terms that suit the notion that there is an equal non-judgemental relationship, where one part facilitates the learning of the other, is that of counsellor and counselled. The continuum from directive to non-directive illustrates the kind of skill we need to develop. It is important that the person reflecting is supported rather than advised, counselled rather than judged.

Carnell and Lodge (2009) put their focus on listening skills in particular:

> Helping someone review their progress and achievement requires the skills of active listening and appropriate questioning and prompting. Active listening requires respect, sincerity and genuineness. It involves paraphrasing, prompting and probing. It needs judgment about the use of open, closed and leading questions and when to move forward. Although the tutor speaks very little, they will be concentrating hard on listening, checking their physical responses, monitoring the progress of the review and deciding when to move on.

> The learners' contributions grow as they develop a shared language with which to describe their learning through talking about learning with each other and with teachers.

Establishing Structure and Ground Rules (Including Pairings)

It might be important, however, to establish the parameters for this kind of relationship. It is important that this is not an opportunity for personal matters. The focus questions should help here to structure the kind of interaction. There is, of course, a dual role for the interaction. Sometimes it is helpful to shift from being facilitator to be a collaborator – suggesting ideas, sharing experiences and offering suggestions about ways forward in order to develop from reflection into action. This is quite a difficult role and it is important to keep it in proportion. If the counselling role represents 90 per cent of the interaction, then being a peer collaborator should take no more than the other 10 per cent.

This is represented as a see-saw because, with the best will in the world, it is extremely difficult to keep silent when the other person is grappling with something and you know you have ideas to help. It is important to acknowledge that whilst the counselling role is beneficial and certainly helps the person to 'work it out for themselves', there is still scope for the constructivist role: 'let's work this out together'; and even the tutor role: 'I think I can suggest something that might help you as it seems to work for me.'

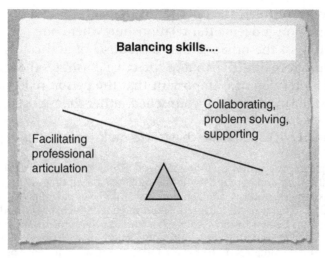

Figure 4.3
Source: Tarrant (2008)

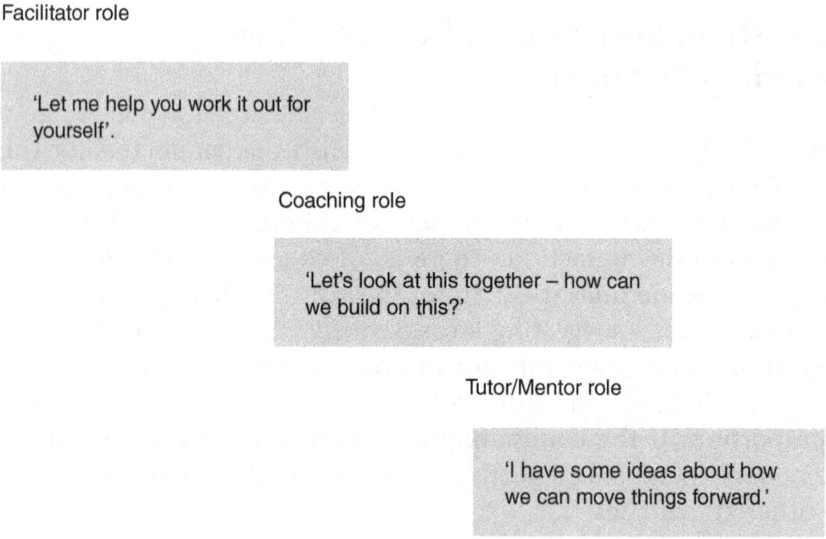

Facilitator role

'Let me help you work it out for yourself'.

Coaching role

'Let's look at this together – how can we build on this?'

Tutor/Mentor role

'I have some ideas about how we can move things forward.'

Figure 4.4   The way the relationship might shift during a peer learning interaction

Developing a Structure to Support the Interactions

There are different ways to approach this and to a certain extent it will depend on your situation and context.

Individual

As an individual wishing to introduce this approach, you will need a high degree of commitment and some willing colleagues. It will be important to impress upon them what it is you are trying to achieve. Initially, you would want to offer the service to them, offering to facilitate whilst they reflect and articulate those reflections to you. Thereafter, having modelled the process, and armed with some focus questions such as those listed earlier in this chapter, they can begin to practise the role of facilitating your reflections. The process will need some practice, however the benefits will motivate you and others involved. Once a few interactions have taken place, the word will spread and you should have more of your colleagues wanting to be involved.

Small group

If you can begin with a group, the task becomes easier. As a group, you should discuss what you want to get out of the process and your understanding of how it works, and agree a programme of interactions. It is important to schedule several sessions on a regular basis early on, say once a week or fortnight. It is important to discuss the kind of questions that might be useful in your context and to add to the list anything you find useful. Again, it is important to clarify the role of each participant and then develop your skills through actually doing it. As discussed above, the more you do it the easier it gets and the more beneficial it becomes for each participant.

Staff group

With a larger group, you can have a more formal structure. Recently, I conducted a workshop in a primary school with around 20 staff. I began with a short lecture establishing what the scheme was about and why it was beneficial. I then modelled how to conduct an interaction, before getting staff to have a go for themselves. We then discussed the kind of questions that might be appropriate to their situation. I ended my session by inviting staff that were interested in being involved to volunteer. Surprisingly, everyone put up their hands! After that, dates were set and pairings established for the first round of interactions. Staff made a commitment initially to meet with someone at least twice in one school term.

It was made clear in that context that the interactions were designed to support professional interaction and reflection and were not to be used as a management tool. The only documentation and evidence requested was that the pairings had actually met. Such a climate of trust and professional responsibility suggests that the staff here will be free to reflect, try new things and have some authentic and relevant professional development in the future.

Whole organization or ITE student group

The introduction of this approach into a larger organization would follow similar lines to those described above for a staff group. However, it might require a more careful structuring of the pairings and the arrangements for them to meet and conduct their interactions.

For example, at Strathclyde University some students were involved in a pilot study into 'peer evaluation' (Kennedy and Allan, 2009). Although significantly different to professional articulation, with more emphasis on being two-way in its peer discussion, it did work on similar lines. Students worked in collaborative trios on placement in schools.

> That the students were familiar with the conditions which promote collaborative practice is clear from their decision, taken before going on placement, that they meet to *establish basic ground rules* (Student B), the key features of which included:
>
> - each student would receive two visits from peers;
>
> - two whole days of the placement would be given over to peer assessment activities with all three students being observed on each of the days;
>
> - the observations would be carried out with pairs observing the third member of the trio;
>
> - the existing diagnostic codes in addition to the benchmark framework used by university tutors would provide the basis for analysing teaching and providing feedback;
>
> - discussions would be held at the end of the day and written reports sent to each other within a week;
>
> - the focus for the observation would not be determined by the student to be observed; rather the observers could observe holistically and decide on the focus areas;
>
> - the focus for the second visit would begin with the action points given in the first feedback;
>
> - documentation of the process would include a rationale for the process negotiated, written feedback to peers authored in pairs, and a reflective personal/professional response. (Kennedy and Allan, 2009: 9)

This approach is different from the peer learning approach advocated by this book. It has many strengths but does not allow for the kind of professional articulations which are personal to the person reflecting or the ownership of the learning in the way described elsewhere in this book. It also relies rather heavily on students 'being observed', and, as stated earlier, there are many convincing arguments that there is as much value in having the interaction when you haven't seen the other person teach as there are arguments for this traditional mode of observation and feedback.

At the University of Edinburgh, students set up their own partners for placement. Whilst out in schools, they then arrange two peer learning interactions each. The first involves one student visiting the other person's placement school. They observe a lesson before having the learning interaction. Later on in the placement, they hold another interaction where they have not observed the teaching. This allows the students to develop their experience by seeing practice in more than one school per placement. It enables them to see other contexts and to be able to 'picture the scene' when they hold the interaction where they do not witness the lesson. After these interactions, the students write up what they learned about themselves as a learner and as a teacher in their professional portfolio along with other reflections on their practice.

In an interview with two post-graduate diploma students, one reported:

> Whether you are observed first will fulfil different criteria. Having someone in the classroom watching you is good in one way: they would be at the same level of development, but not judgmental of you, supportive. They can see what happens in class and how the pupils interact.

> But it would be just as good in different ways if they didn't observe the lesson because you would have to think through and to explain what you did in more detail, you wouldn't take it for granted that the other person knew what you meant. (Sue, PGDE student)

It is very important to stress this connection between the reflection and the next steps for teaching and learning. Professionals do reflect, they do adapt their practice. What this approach tries to encourage is to consolidate this learning by having the opportunity to articulate it. Having done so, they can then consider the 'so what?' questions. It is not enough to simply notice that something went well, or went badly, it is essential to move on from that to say, 'So what? Next time I'm going to...'

Accountability Tools

In any professional context, management will be keen to see evidence of the reflection and these 'next steps'. They will want to know that time invested produces some positive impact on practice. Inevitably, this might mean that there is a desire for some tangible evidence that the peer learning interaction has taken place. It would also be important to have some written record of 'progress made'. By 'progress', I mean evidence of the reflection informing practice – either in terms of doing what works well more often, or in terms of changes in practice in order to improve performance. This means that some kind of record of the session, the realizations in the session about practice, and the planned next steps and professional support needs all need to be documented in some way. (We will return to this in more detail in the next chapter.)

Moral Considerations

Any counselling approach to reflection will need to take into consideration the fact that, by definition, counselling includes an element of a personal nature. It is, therefore, important to ensure that the ground rules are established and adhered to. The whole point of the reflection is that it is of a professional nature. It may be that other elements of professional, or indeed, personal life could encroach into this dialogue. However, having a professional focus and a bank of appropriate questions with which to structure the session should help to keep on track. 'It is not always "safe" but can be threatening as you question your practice. It is about being professionally self-critical without being destructive and overly negative' (Ghaye and Ghaye, 1998: 3).

If other, more personal information does come out in these interactions, it is essential that the person doing the facilitation is comfortable with handling the session and can deal with what is discussed in a confidential and sensitive manner. Thereafter, it may be important for the facilitator to have someone else with whom to share how the session went and how it made them feel, without, of course, disclosing any private/personal details that might have been confided in them.

Challenges and Possible Solutions

There are many good reasons to reflect on your professional practice. There are many good reasons to get involved in a peer learning interaction in order to reflect on and articulate your developing understanding of yourself as a professional and your practice as part of a much bigger organization. However, there are also many reasons not to do these things. Many professionals will say that they have no time for such 'new' initiatives. Others will say that they do reflect anyway and do not need another approach. Then there will be those who say they firmly believe in the value of reflection and that this is a great way to go about it, yet not actually get involved themselves. There are also those who feel uncomfortable about the idea of sharing their reflections with someone else, and others who feel threatened by any move which looks like a management initiative to make them even more accountable. 'These can be occasions when, in trying to facilitate a reflective conversation, we sense that there is (or might be) a hidden agenda that might take quite a bit of teasing out' (Ghaye, 2011: 43). It is important when trying to initiate something like peer learning in your context to make sure that you counter these arguments.

Reasons why people do not formally reflect in a professional manner:

1 I don't have enough time.

2 I'm doing it already.

3 It makes me feel threatened.

4 I'm too busy.

5 I don't trust you.

6 It's just a guise for checking up on me.

7 I don't want to be made to feel vulnerable and inadequate.

8 I have too much to do already.

9 I can and do reflect all the time, I don't need anybody else.

10 Nobody makes me do it so I never quite get around to it.

Clearly, there is much written in this book about the need for there to be trust between participants. I have also stressed the principle that the approach is not about a topdown management accountability agenda; it is important that the agenda belongs to the individual.

Time is an important obstacle, yet the peer learning interactions advocated in this book take up only around 30 minutes.

The task is to convince people that this is time well spent. 'Nobody makes me do it' and 'I'm too busy' are responses that really sum up the challenges to introducing this approach. In Initial Teacher Education, we have the luxury of making such professional encounters an essential component of courses. Students have to do it, at least once, for every school placement. It is hoped that having done so, they might overcome many of the reasons *not to* participate and then go on and continue reflecting in this way long after it is imposed on them by the university.

In schools and other professions, it might be a matter of management, 'persuading' staff to try the approach for a while until they realize that it isn't about an imposed agenda, accountability or any other sinister threat, but instead it is a useful approach in which they themselves will feel very much in control.

One of the other fears for a lot of professionals and students is that of having someone observe them in action when they do not feel confident to have them there. This applies to the professional as well as to the novice.

Staff who feel threatened and worried about change should be reassured that they can become involved, and benefit from articulating their reflections without ever having to have someone coming in to see them perform.

This is one of the strengths of this approach and one that sets it apart from other reflective approaches. The act of describing your own practice is vital to the scheme and represents an opportunity for those who still feel uneasy about having an observer looking at their practice.

However, it is true to say that the relationship between the partners reflecting can have a big impact upon its success. For example, a more experienced or dominant partner might make the other person less likely to engage fully in honest and frank reflection.

In an interview with two PGDE students, they reported:

> Sue: I think if you were doing it with somebody experienced, it would be different as well; somebody that had been teaching for a while. You may not feel

a power relationship in that they were judging you, but you would be inclined to defer to their experience and feel that what they said had more credence than what you had thought yourself.

Kelly: I think they might be thinking 'I wouldn't do it that way', in a judgmental way, whereas I was thinking 'oh I wouldn't have thought to do it like that' when Sue was doing it. I was willing to learn from her, whereas with a more experienced person it might be more of a one-way learning.

Sue: Indeed they might close down your options. Because you might feel in awe of them and think, 'oh well if that's how a more experienced person does it, that's the way to do it', you might feel that that's the way you 'should do it', whereas seeing a peer enables you to look with a more open mind to other possibilities.

Certainly, there are many advantages in holding the interactions with someone at a similar stage of development. Whether this is with students in ITE or fellow professionals out in the field, there will need to be some activities devised to enable effective working partnerships to develop. The implications of this lead us back once again to the question of 'time'. Time is indeed one of the most difficult challenges. However, it is also important to stress that the actual peer learning interaction can be held in a 30-minute session. This can be at the end of the day, or during a non-contact period throughout the day. The biggest challenge is getting staff to commit to being involved in the first place. Once they have tried this for a few sessions, they can then see the personal and professional value of the interactions. They also realize that time is not in fact a problem.

In ITE and in larger organizations, it is easier to enable participants to see the value of the interactions. This can be done by making peer learning a prerequisite element of the programme. In smaller institutions like schools, it is up to the management to get staff involved, to convince them of its worth and then to facilitate its organization so that there is space, time and encouragement for meetings to take place. Without such support, there is the need for a good deal of commitment from those involved in order to make it a success.

Earlier in the discussion, we touched upon the question of whether to observe the other person before the reflective interaction or to pass on the observation, instead relying on the person reflecting to describe their practice in a reflective way. Each approach has its advantages and disadvantages, as discussed elsewhere in this book. Below, we will look at how we might set up either of these approaches.

To observe first or not?

Peer Learning *with* Observation

Step 1

Pair up with someone else. Ideally, this should be someone at the same stage of development, i.e. two students from the same year, two professionals who are new to the organization/profession, two of the more experienced members of staff. As Brufee (1997: 42–7) suggests, 'the educational effects of peer tutoring, both in the long and short run, are contingent upon the degree to which the tutor and tutee are really peers'. For Amitt (1997), 'in the realm of peer tutoring, equality means two things: both tutor and student believe that they bring important skills and information to the session'.

In the article 'Collaborative learning theory and peer tutoring practice', author Alice Gillam (undated, 53–65) states: 'Making sense should be seen as an active and creative process of jointly constructed inter-pretations, an act of collaborative meaning making.'

Step 2

Make arrangements to visit and to observe your peer in action. Remember that you will both know the kind of questions that will be used in the reflection interaction. It may be that you wish to have additional questions to draw out something that you wish to focus upon in the interaction, i.e. in a teaching context there might be a desire to investigate different ways of getting the attention of the class. An agreement would be made to include questions like:

> What strategies did you use to get the attention of the class?
>
> Which methods worked best? Why was this?
>
> How might you make more consistent use of the successful approaches?
>
> Can you suggest ways of improving the approaches that were less successful?

If the questions are established in advance, there should be no surprises and both participants can focus on the observation and the interaction with confidence.

Step 3

Agree where physically the observation will take place and what the role will be of the person observing, i.e. where will you stand/sit? Will you be introduced to the class? Will you be taking notes, etc.? Agree how long the observation will last and what will happen at the end.

Step 4

It may not be possible or desirable to have the peer learning interaction immediately after the observation. It may be that it takes place at the end of the working day, or even on a day that follows. There are some advantages in there being some delay – the participants have more time to reflect and to consider the lesson in the light of agreed questions, for example. However, it is better if the gap is not too long, otherwise things can be forgotten and the reflection will lose some of its impact.

Step 5

Make sure that the interaction takes place in a location that is comfortable and free from interruption. Try to reserve around 45 minutes for the interaction if possible. Even though 30 minutes is the optimum length for such an interaction, it is best to have extra time built in if possible, so that there isn't a sense of rushing things at the end. You may wish to record the interaction for reference later, or to have support notes or a paper trail. Alternatively, you may decide that one of you will make brief notes during the interaction. Often, it is useful if it is the person doing the articulation who makes brief notes at the end of the session. Later in the book, there are pro formas for collecting the reflections and outlining actions to be taken, should these be required.

Step 6

Begin the interaction. Use the focus questions plus any additional ones that you have added. Even though you have witnessed what happened in practice, it is important to try to get the person articulating *to describe* what happened as if you weren't there. It is often this description that enables the reflections to unearth things in everyday routines that is surprisingly remarkable.

You should also try to encourage the person reflecting to talk about the positive elements of their practice: What went well? Why was this? How had you prepared so that this success was possible? How might you apply this knowledge and understanding in another element of your practice, i.e. if the hands-on practical materials helped the participants to understand and grasp difficult concepts, might similar materials help in other situations?

Interactions that begin the reflection by describing what happened usually unearth interesting reflections about what went well, or went badly. However, sometimes this is not the case and the role of the facilitator is to try to guide the reflector to consider what it was about their practice that was pleasing/frustrating/surprising/remarkable.

It is important to get at the questions that encourage reflection on the nature of professionalism such as:

What did you learn about yourself as a teacher?

What did you learn about being a professional?

What did you learn about learning and teaching?

What did you learn about your own ability to ...?

As discussed elsewhere in this book, it is not your role to offer advice or personal experiences in order to support the articulations. Sometimes silence is necessary, no matter how uncomfortable you might find it, in order that the person reflecting really gets to grips with the situation being considered.

One piece of self advice is worth a hundred tips from someone else!

It is important to actively listen to what the person reflecting has to say. It would be all too easy to simply interrogate them with the agreed questions one after another with no contingent response. It is more effective and more important that the facilitator enables the other person to reflect and to consider the question in detail. The facilitator should listen and try to 'piggy-back' on what is said, building a more natural discourse. The aim is for a professional monologue for the person reflecting. Therefore, intervention, interaction and lots of questions should be discouraged.

It is important to focus on the one lesson/experience and to try to get them to analyse in detail why the lesson is significant to them. It is often easy to give up and move on if the other person seems unsure or reluctant. This is when effective questioning, wait time and active listening really come into play. If they have chosen this particular experience to discuss, there is usually a good reason for it, so it is important to allow space for them to reflect and articulate precisely what it is that is significant for them.

Step 7 (next steps)

At some point in the interaction, it is important to try to recap on what has been said and to turn to action points. For example:

Is there some change to practice that is going to be beneficial, arising out of this reflection?

Is there something new to try another time?

Is there something that worked well that you would wish to repeat another time or in another context?

These action points may form the basis for a record of the interaction and have some relevance for the next interaction. Revisiting such action points can help to build trust, to support a sense of progress and professional development and can help to identify any themes that inform other forms of professional and institutional development, i.e. the difficulties you are wrestling with are common to others in your workplace and suggest the need for institutional change or some in-service provision to support a number of professionals together.

Peer Learning *without* Observation

For the reasons cited already in this book, it is important to experience some peer learning interactions at times when there was no observation to inform the discussion. Such interactions encourage the person articulating to reflect and describe what happened and in doing so to realize something significant about the routine as well as the extraordinary. The process for this is similar to the method already outlined for peer learning with observation.

I have chosen to reproduce the process here despite the repetition of what has been said as I imagine that many readers will refer back to this structure and will not want to read both sections.

Step 1

Pair up with someone else. Ideally, this should be someone at the same stage of development, i.e. two students from the same year, two professionals who are new to the organization/profession, two of the more experienced members of staff.

Step 2

Make arrangements to meet up for the peer learning interaction. Remember that you will both know the kind of questions that will be used in the reflection interaction.

It may be that you wish to have additional questions to draw out something that you wish to focus upon in the interaction, i.e. in a teaching context there might be a desire to investigate different ways of getting the attention of the class.

An agreement to include questions like, for example:

What strategies did you use to get the attention of the class?

Which methods worked best? Why was this?

How might you make more consistent use of the successful approaches?

Can you suggest ways of improving the approaches that were less successful?

Step 3

Make sure that the interaction takes place in a location that is comfortable and free from interruption. Try to reserve around 45 minutes for the interaction if possible. You may wish to record the interaction for reference later, or to support notes or a paper trail. Alternatively, you may decide that one of you will make brief notes during the interaction. Often, it is useful if it is the person doing the articulation who makes brief notes at the end of the session. Later in the book, there are pro formas for collecting the reflections and outlining actions to be taken.

Step 4

It may not be possible or desirable to have the peer learning interaction immediately after the lesson to be discussed. It may be that it takes place at the end of the working day, or even on a day that follows. There are some advantages in there being some delay – the participants have more time to reflect and to consider the lesson in the light of agreed questions, for example. However, it is better if the gap is not too long, otherwise things can be forgotten and the reflection will lose some of its impact.

Step 5

Make sure that the interaction takes place in a location that is comfortable and free from interruption. Try to reserve around 45 minutes for the interaction if possible. You may wish to record the interaction for reference later, or to have support notes or a paper trail. Alternatively, you may decide that one of you will make brief notes during the interaction. Often, it is useful if it is the person doing the articulation who makes brief notes at the end of the session. Later in the book, there are proformas for collecting the reflections and outlining actions to be taken.

Step 6

Begin the interaction. Use the focus questions plus any additional ones that you have added. It is important to try to get the person articulating *to describe* what happened. It is often this description that enables the reflections to unearth things in everyday routines that are surprisingly remarkable.

You should also try to encourage the person reflecting to talk about the positive elements of their practice: What went well? Why was this? How had you prepared so that this success was possible? How might you apply this knowledge and understanding in another element of your practice, i.e. if the hands-on practical materials helped the participants to understand and grasp difficult concepts, might similar materials help in other situations?

Interactions that begin with reflection by describing what happened usually unearth interesting reflections about what went well, or went badly. However, sometimes this is not the case and the role of the facilitator is to try to guide the reflector to consider what it was about their practice that was pleasing/frustrating/surprising/remarkable.

It is important to get at questions that encourage reflection on the nature of professionalism such as:

What did you learn about yourself as a teacher?

What did you learn about being a professional?

What did you learn about learning and teaching?

What did you learn about your own ability to ...?

As discussed elsewhere in this book, it is not your role to offer advice or personal experiences in order to support the articulations. Sometimes silence is necessary, no matter how uncomfortable you might find it, in order that the person reflecting really gets to grips with the situation being considered.

> One piece of self advice is worth a hundred tips from someone else.

It is important to actively listen to what the person reflecting has to say. It would be all too easy to simply interrogate them with the agreed questions one after another with no contingent response. It is more effective and more important that the facilitator enables the other person to reflect and to consider the question in detail. The facilitator should listen and try to 'piggy-back' on what is said, building a more natural discourse. The aim is for a professional monologue for the person reflecting. Therefore, intervention, interaction and lots of questions should be discouraged.

It is important to focus on the one lesson/experience and to try to get them to analyse in detail why the lesson is significant to them. It is often easy to give up and move on if the other person seems unsure or reluctant. This is when effective questioning, wait time and active listening really come into play. If they have chosen this particular experience to discuss, there is usually a good reason for it, so it is important to allow space for them to reflect and articulate precisely what it is that is significant for them.

Step 7 (next steps)

At some point in the interaction, it is important to try to recap on what has been said and to turn to action points. For example:

Is there some change to practice that is going to be beneficial, arising out of this reflection?

Is there something new to try another time?

Is there something that worked well that you would wish to repeat another time or in another context?

These action points may form the basis for a record of the interaction and have a relevance for the next interaction. Revisiting such action points can help to build trust, to support a sense of progress and professional development and can help to identify any themes that inform other forms of professional and institutional development, i.e. the difficulties you are wrestling with are common to others in your workplace and suggest the need for institutional change or some in-service provision to support a number of professionals together.

 Summary

In this chapter, we have considered ways of introducing peer learning interactions into the workplace. There are detailed outlines on how an individual, small group or larger organization might get involved in using this approach towards professional reflection. We looked in some detail at the kind of skills and questions needed and how one might approach these. We also looked at the importance of relationship and trust. A detailed structure for introducing the approach was discussed, as well as ways of recording progress so that reflection can be translated into development action. We explored some of the reasons why reflection on a regular basis is not more widely practised and considered some strategies for overcoming these obstacles.

 Questions for Reflection

- Think about how you might get involved in this kind of reflection. Is there someone with whom you might work as a peer learning partner? Does your school, college or workplace have scope for introducing such a scheme?
- Look at the reflective questions – which of these would be suitable for you at your stage of development in your profession? Add to them and adapt any that would need to be re-worded.
- Find someone to try them out with. Get them to focus on something that they have been doing recently that is for some reason

(Continued)

(Continued)

memorable to them. Remember when asking the questions to try to enable them to do most of the talking and not to give your own opinions and experiences. You might find it difficult not to give advice and personal anecdotes, but try as far as you can to let them 'work things out for themselves'.

- Afterwards, reflect on how the session went. How good were the questions? How effective were your questioning techniques and silences? What about your body language and eye contact?
- Then change roles and get your partner to facilitate for you. Afterwards, discuss how the experience felt and how you might improve things another time.
- Think about the obstacles for you in terms of regular reflection. What might get in the way? What do you need to overcome these challenges?

Further Reading

- Alexander, R. (2002) *Good Practice: More than a Mantra?* In Pollard, A. (ed) *Readings For Reflective Teaching.* Continuum: London. pp. 159–64.
- Ghaye, A. and Ghaye, K. (1998) *Teaching and Learning through Critical Reflective Practice.* London: David Fulton, Chapter 1.
- Moon, J. A. (1999) *Reflection in Learning and Professional Development.* London: RoutledgeFalmer, Chapter 5.
- Moyles, J., Suschitzky, S. and Chapman, L. (1998) *The Challenges of Effective Mentoring.* In Pollard, A. (ed) (2002) *Readings For Reflective Teaching.* Continuum: London. Reading 16.4 (p343).
- Samson, J. and Pollard, A. (2002) *Readings For Reflective Teaching.* Continuum: London. Reading 2.1 (p18).

References

Annett, N. (1997) *Collaboration and the Peer Tutor: Characteristics, Constraints, and Ethical Considerations in the Writing Center.* Available at: http://writing2.richmond.edu/training/fall97/nanne/peer.html

Brufee, K., cited in Annett, N. (1997) *Collaboration and the Peer Tutor: Characteristics, Constraints, and Ethical Considerations in the Writing Center.* http://writing2.richmond.edu/training/fall97/nanne/peer.html

Brufee, K. (1987) *The Act of Collaborative Learning: Making the Most of Knowledgeable Peers.* Baltimore: The John Hopkins University Press.

Carnell, E. and Lodge, C. (2009) *Supporting Effective Learning.* London: Sage.

Department for Education (DFE) (2011) *Professional Standard for Teachers: Professional Attributes.* London: DFE.

Elmore, R. F. (2007) *School Reform from the Inside Out.* Cambridge, MA: Harvard Education Press.

Ghaye, A. and Ghaye, K. (1998) *Teaching and Learning through Critical Reflective Practice.* London: David Fulton.

Ghaye, T. (2011) *Teaching and Learning Through Reflective Practice: A Practical Guide for Positive Action.* Oxen: Routledge.

Gillam, A. M. (undated) 'Collaborative learning theory and peer tutoring practice', in J. A. Mullin and R. Wallace (eds) *Intersections: Theory–Practice in the Writing Centre.* Illinois: The National Council of Teachers of English. pp. 53–65.

Kennedy, A. and Allan, J. (2009) '"The assessor and the assessed": learning from students' reflections on peer-evaluation,' *Journal of Teacher Education and Teachers' Work*, 1 (1).

Laboskey, V. 'A conceptual framework for reflection in pre-service teachers education', in Calderhead, J. and Gates, P. (eds) *Conceptualising Reflection in Teacher Development.* London: The Falmer Press.

The Scottish Government (2001) *Quality Assurance in Initial Teacher Education: The Standard for Initial Teacher Education in Scotland – Benchmark Information.* Edinburgh: The Scottish Government.

Van Manon, M. (1991) *The Tact of Teaching.* New York: The State of New York Press.

5

How does reflective practice fit into the 'big picture'?

Chapter Overview

This chapter will evaluate where peer learning might fit as part of a raft of measures designed to both support and develop reflective practice and also fit into the need to monitor and evaluate the performance of adults in school. It strives to consider the emerging professional as a valued member of the community of practice who has something to contribute as well as something to learn.

- Kinds of accountability
- How is it currently done?
- Peer learning and professional review
- Paper trails
- Into action
- Is there another way? Can we integrate some of these approaches?
- Progression: a raft of approaches

Whilst it is desirable to introduce approaches which get away from the accountability agendas and from the power relationships inherent in 'expert' observing and feeding back to the 'apprentice', it would be naïve to believe that this would be enough to ensure a high standard of professionalism and of learning and teaching in our schools. It is true that some check is necessary, some way of monitoring performance, establishing and maintaining standards, and supporting professional development. There are many ways in which this can be done, but the philosophy of this book suggests that there is a way of developing practice, making people accountable, and yet supporting and enabling them to develop in a more positive and less threatening way. Having ownership and direction coming from the professional who recognizes their own strengths and their need to develop is much more powerful than the person who feels judged and pushed along some development unwillingly.

A model of reflection and professional development which is contrived, and involves staff opting for some elements of development or in-service training because of external agendas, may only result in some kind of enforced development. Such an attitude does not bode well for professional development. It is much better if the desire to improve, to re-train, to develop, comes from a genuine, authentic desire to progress – with a clear and specific goal based upon professional reflection.

It is this connection between reflective practice and moving towards professional development that is most powerful. In an ideal scenario, this would happen without any need for accountability or a top-down approach which directs staff towards what they should be doing. However, in order to support those who find this approach challenging, and for those in authority who need evidence that there is professional reflection and a clear plan for development, there is a need for something more. 'It is like standing in front of the mirror, with someone else who can help you see things about you, that have become too familiar for you to notice' (Clutterbuck and Megginson, 1999: 17).

Kinds of Accountability

In Chapter 1, we looked at what was meant by professionalism. In it we established that this was to do with attitudes and values. It was to do with having the skills and aptitudes for the job and a professional disposition towards the execution of your duties. A reflective approach towards your professional practice may be enough to convince you that you are, indeed, a competent practitioner. However, there will always be the need for this to be demonstrated, performed and evidenced for others in your profession. Management need to maintain standards: standards in the workplace, standards in the profession. By definition, professionals need to be made accountable in order for their expertise to be valued and recognized.

In order to consider the link between professionalism and accountability, it is important to consider what we mean by accountability. We should consider:

Who is made accountable?

Who they are accountable to?

How are they made accountable?

What are the benefits of being made accountable?

What are the drawbacks/challenges?

Who is made accountable?

In every profession, there are rigorous ways of making staff accountable. All staff are monitored in some way, though generally there is an emphasis on reaching targets, increasing productivity or improving results. Even in teaching there has, in the past, been some emphasis on the ability to 'get them through the tests'. Formal accountability comes in several forms, but usually in the shape of an annual review of progress that results in targets being set for the year to follow.

Informally, accountability may be supported via data and evidence such as looking at what is achieved, produced or gained in the workplace by the professional. In high schools, this may well be tied in with exam results. However, teaching has many less tangible goals and achievements to be taken into account. These can only be monitored through a clear understanding of the context, the pupils and the challenges faced by the teacher being monitored. Other aspects of informal assessment may be achieved through the collection of data from plans, evaluations, pupil workbooks and exam results.

In teaching, this can be a subjective process as there is so much of the performance that is regulated by the success of the pupil–teacher relationship. In such circumstances, it is important that the person assessed has the opportunity to voice their opinions regarding what is happening in practice and how this might impact on 'performance' in practice.

Wildman and Niles observed that systematic reflection on teaching required a sound ability to understand classroom events in an objective manner. They suggest that teachers rarely have the time or opportunities to view their own or the teaching of others in an objective manner. Further observations revealed the tendency of teachers to evaluate events rather than to review the contributory factors in a considered manner. (Cited in Moon, 1999, p68.)

In the past, there has been a good deal of stress caused by 'one-off' inspections, where someone is brought in to take a 'snap-shot' of practice and then deliver a judgement on the effectiveness of the professional. In recent times, there has been more dialogue and a better understanding of the significance of the context and some of the background factors to the professional's performance. However, the nervousness of being observed and a suspicion of those doing the monitoring have meant that there is considerable resistance to formal methods of accountability. This may explain why formal observations and professional review do not occur very often. This in turn means that when they do, the stakes are higher and the participants less experienced in terms of performing for the occasion, reflecting and then articulating professionally their strengths and development needs. Certainly, there is little evidence yet of what Wildman and Niles (1987: 25–31) refer to as 'a systematic reflection on teaching'.

In particular, for students in Initial Teacher Education there has historically been an emphasis on the one-off, observed lesson from the tutor who comes to visit from Faculty. The stakes are high and this can often be reflected in the performance of the student. Often the nerves generated by the poor student can be spread to the pupils; the erstwhile angelic class suddenly find themselves twitching and demonstrating 'devilish tendencies' during the lesson. Such a background does not afford the best opportunity for the abilities of the student teacher to emerge.

In research done by Aileen Kennedy and Jim Allan of the University of Strathclyde, it was found that:

> Although the observational visits undertaken by university tutors take up only a small fraction of any student teacher's teaching time, they are generally regarded by all concerned as highly significant.

> During a PGCE year, frequently characterised by intensity of experience, both positive and negative, impressing one's tutor plays a perhaps disproportionate role in the personal and professional transformations and changes likely to occur during the course. (Kennedy and Allan, 2009: 6)

Who are we accountable to?

To ourselves. We have a professional responsibility to execute our duties to the best of our abilities. Regardless of other agents and organizational constructs, we are ultimately responsible to ourselves. Consequently, a reflective approach like that espoused by this book, will provide opportunities to consider how well things are going and possible ways of making improvements.

To our clients. In any profession, there will be the receivers of our efforts, our clients. In teaching this means the pupils. Our responsibility towards them is an important indicator of how we are performing professionally. We are accountable to them in as much as they will be the first to benefit or suffer from our performance. Parents too are included in this. The relationship between teacher and parent is essential in developing the best approach for pupils in and out of school. Teachers are made accountable by parents and it is important to maintain good communication with them. In terms of reflective practice, it is important that parents see the tangible evidence that your reflection is being translated into improvements in practice.

To our management and our employers. It is essential that management in any profession have evidence that the workforce is delivering a high standard of service and that values, principles and actions are representative of the profession. There are many structures that seek to maintain standards and provide evidence of this and I will return to this later.

To our colleagues and fellow professionals. We are accountable towards our colleagues in as much as we strive together to represent our profession in the best way that we can. Falling down on standards or performance has a negative effect on all of the profession. We are accountable to fellow professionals in as much as we jointly represent established values, attitudes and conduct. Therefore, it is vital that we are able to reflect on our practice and to provide evidence that the standard is being met.

How are we made accountable?

In Initial Teacher Education, the standard is set by the government and the Teaching Council and the monitoring is done by the ITE tutor and the school mentor. There is also a role played by the school management team in assessing against the standard. Once qualified, teachers still have to achieve the standard for full registration. Again, monitoring is done by the mentor and also the school management team. Beyond this, the head teacher has a role in monitoring progress and maintaining standards of teaching in the school. Overriding all of this, the government has its inspectors to maintain standards and to monitor consistency across the different schools and authorities.

In the Donaldson report (2010) in Scotland, setting out the findings of the *Review of Teacher Education* (The Scottish Government, 2011), there is a reference to reflection and professionalism in other professions. It is useful to refer to how another profession has addressed the need for all aspects of professionalism to be developed through practice. In *Tomorrow's Doctors: Outcomes and Standards for Undergraduate Medical Education* (General Medical Council, 2009), this notion is placed clearly at the heart of professionalism:

> It is not enough for a clinician to act as a practitioner in their own discipline. They must act as partners to their colleagues, accepting shared accountability for the service provided to patients. They are also expected to offer leadership, and to work with others to change systems when it is necessary for the benefit of patients. (Donaldson, 2010: 42)

Clearly, it is not just in teaching that the value and impact of mentoring, partnership and reflection are undergoing some scrutiny. The report goes on to state: 'Scotland is not alone in needing to improve the quality, relevance and impact of Continuous Professional Development. Across the world, there is concern about the impact of Continuous Professional Development and teacher quality on outcomes for young people' (Donaldson, 2010: 67).

What are the benefits of being made accountable?

As already mentioned, it is important that standards are maintained in any profession. There is a benefit to the management and the institution, to the clients or customers and to the profession as a whole. There is also the element of accountability that informs. When another respected professional has viewed our professional practice, it gives us validation – validation that we are doing the right things; validation that our own self-evaluation is somewhere close to the truth.

Feedback from other professionals enables us to take stock, to look more objectively at our practice and to consider ways of enhancing and improving what we do. Without any kind of accountability, we might become complacent and work in a vacuum where we are unaware of how others are doing things and how our own performance might compare with theirs.

Without accountability, we might lack the drive to improve, we might miss out on the opportunity to share our own good practice with others. When our manager or external body comes to view our work, it somehow gives what we are doing some added credibility. This acknowledgement of the value of what we do is part of our professional identity and helps to develop our professional values.

The view in this book, however, is that through regular reflective practice, we will be more able to articulate just how we see ourselves and our practice. We will be more self-aware, and feel more a part of the ongoing professional process rather than feel like a 'victim' of judgement from others. Moreover, we will be better equipped to justify our practice and to communicate what we have been doing and want to do to continue to improve as professionals.

What are the drawbacks/challenges?

Laudable as all of this is, there are still those who resist the measures that make us accountable. Some are concerned, threatened even, by an institution that puts pressure on them to continually prove themselves. Others see the interference of management and its methods to make them accountable, intrusive and something that gets in the way of the performance of their duties. Some, indeed, find that the very thought of someone coming to observe them going about their duties is enough to unnerve them so much that their performance suffers. Much depends on who is doing the observing and how it is done. In teaching, it is often the university tutor or head teacher who has to make staff accountable. This can cause a lot of stress and anxiety for those who are expected to demonstrate their worth.

In the report from the Scottish Government, it was found that:

> There can be a tension between the mentoring and the assessment function that many mentors also carry out. This can affect the extent to which new teachers genuinely engage in coaching and mentoring conversations where they reveal weaknesses because of the consequences for the formal assessments their mentor undertakes. Some probationers also commented that they did not want to challenge or disagree with their mentor, even when they disagreed with their teaching approaches, for fear of any repercussions. A few new teachers reported that a priority for them in successfully completing their induction year was maintaining a positive relationship with their mentor. (Donaldson, 2010: 52)

The challenge is to have systems in place that support the practitioner but at the same time provide management opportunities to see good professional practice and establish evidence that staff are performing and developing adequately.

One of the goals of this book is that both emerging and established professionals can be supported in their practice and their reflection so that they are better prepared for any evaluative interaction. The point is that as professionals we want to improve, we want to get better and better. Therefore, opportunities that arise where these professional reflections can be shared and transformed into development action, are going to be beneficial. There will be a big difference between a professional being made accountable occasionally and out of the blue, compared with someone who is accustomed to reflecting on and articulating the strengths and needs associated with their practice on a regular basis.

> ... an important goal is to achieve a greater sense of clarity, rationality and certainty that teaching was done professionally and ethically, and what was done was worthwhile and meaningful... it is through reflective conversations that our established and existing knowledge that guides our teaching can be undone and reorganised to increase its future educational worth. (Ghaye, 2011: 45)

How is it Currently Done?

In initial teacher education?

Emerging professionals are made accountable via a range of assessments – for example, academic essays, presentations and school placements. Students placed in local schools undertake practical experience in the classroom and are evaluated by the class teacher, sometimes additionally by the head teacher and also by a tutor from the university. Traditionally, there was a 'crit lesson' where the tutor would come in to see the student 'perform' a lesson and then provide feedback and a grade.

More recently, tutor visits have become more formative; in Scotland there is no longer a system where students are given grades for their performance. Indeed, for many the stress and anxiety of a tutor visit or formal evaluation was sufficient to impair the quality of the lesson observed. The notion of self-evaluation is becoming more and more evident across the UK, and students are encouraged to pair up with each other and to undergo some peer observations and follow-up discussions about their practice.

How is it currently done in schools?

Certainly, teachers need to get used to being observed. After their ITE experiences, student teachers enter an induction year. During this period, they have a mentor who will support them in school. As part of this mentoring, they will be 'made accountable' in as much as the mentor will observe them teaching, discuss their practice, and ultimately decide if they meet the standard and are competent enough to go on to full registration as a qualified teacher.

This process continues for the rest of the teacher's career. Observation and feedback on performance is a key part of the accountability process in education. Whether it is the university tutor in ITE or the school management team or the HMIE or Ofsted inspection, the approach is generally one of getting the professional to perform their duties under the watchful eye of the 'expert' before receiving feedback and (often) judgement on their performance. These observations can be augmented through additional measures where evidence can be offered as an indicator of the quality of the performance. For example, exercise books, jotters, and other evidence of learning might be collected in and evaluated. Lesson plans, evaluations and exam results all may feature in the attempt to examine the process, as well as the product associated with the teacher's job in the classroom.

As stated earlier, there are many good reasons for making professionals accountable. However, many of the elements above seem to be more about the assessor than the practitioner. The importance of ownership and a sense of wanting to develop practice in a constructive way get rather lost in the desire to make someone accountable and present evidence to support the evaluation.

What this book strives to do is to present some ideas as to how the professionals themselves can have more ownership of the process; how they can set some of the agenda; how they can feel more power to justify themselves and then go on and initiate change for themselves. What is needed though is some way of evidencing how reflective interactions can manifest themselves as action and evidence in a way that will tick the accountability boxes of their masters.

Traditionally, observations may lead to staff being directed towards some kind of CPD or professional development. Such suggestions might be on the basis of what was observed by management, or due to things which are high on the management agenda. However, instead of this contrived or enforced development, how much better would it be if the teacher himself was able to identify and articulate what it is that he needs?

> Overall, there is a lack of conviction about PRD processes across Scotland. Advice issued by the Scottish Executive, 'Guidance on the procedure for professional review and development for teachers in Scotland' (2004), states that PRD should be based on self-evaluation, with teachers encouraged to use professional standards as the main point of reference. A learning cycle was introduced and teachers were asked to consider the impact on learners and their own development as professionals. The requirements for a CPD plan and a CPD record were further exemplified in this important document, but its influence has as yet been limited. (Donaldson, 2010: 72)

This 'lack of conviction' and 'limited influence' of a more frequent, systematic and structured approach perhaps signpost the need for something like the peer learning interactions outlined in this book.

The notion of peer learning interactions, and a pattern of regular sessions where practitioners stop, reflect on and articulate their developing ideas and skills development, before going on to set individual targets and personal development goals, is far removed from the traditional one-off inspection or management observation and feedback. Such a scheme, where reflection happens more frequently, should make each session less stressful and equip those reflecting with the skill, experience and evidence required to effectively go to such a meeting with management with confidence and on a more equal footing.

It is to these annual development meetings that we now turn. Sometimes referred to as Staff Review and Appraisal, they are more commonly renamed Staff Development and Review – in order, no doubt, to move away from the explicit accountability agenda towards more of a supportive, 'development' approach.

Peer Learning and Professional Review

In Scotland, there have been recent developments which acknowledge the importance of professional review. In September 2011, the McCormac Review recommended that: 'All teachers should be engaged in a revitalised process of Professional Review and Personal Development which should be implemented consistently and on a national basis' (McCormac, 2011: 16, Recommendation 2).

The subject of some kind of professional accountability had been on the agenda for some time but this was a clear message to schools that professionalism needed to have a higher profile and that in order to ensure professional development some system needed to be put in place.

Of course, the notion of professional review and development can represent an agenda that is different from the peer learning approach advocated in this book. Indeed, accountability and links to frequent re-accreditation were very much in the mind of McCormac at the time of the review.

There are, of course, big differences between professional development and review meetings, held annually to discuss performance and agree development action, and peer learning articulations. The peer learning approach encourages more frequent sessions where staff can reflect on the specifics of their practice; where they can unravel practice and explore how their performance can develop and grow. These interactions are structured so that participants devise their own agenda without fear of being judged or assessed, and where there is a climate of trust and the freedom to experiment in order to develop. At first sight, these two approaches might seem poles apart. However, it may be that a 'first step' towards the introduction of such a professional review could well be the peer learning approach.

Experience in articulating personal development through peer learning interactions could be beneficial for a number of reasons:

- Staff would feel more confident and able to discuss their professional performance and progress.

- Staff would have a clearer understanding of their own strengths and development needs.

- Such knowledge and confidence would give staff more ownership of the review.

- Staff conducting the reviews would have more experience and understanding of how to go about the process.

It may be that the kind of approach discussed in this book would feed into the more formal once-a-year review where the experiences of many, many peer learning sessions are summarized and distilled into a review of progress and plan of future development. It is true that PRD is also about making professionals more accountable, but the series of peer learning articulations provide a wealth of experience and information with which such assessment can then be informed. Instead of the review being a once-a-year snapshot, it can be based on a more accurate picture of progress and development. 'Other staff, within a school, who contribute to the education of pupils should be entitled to PRPD. These groups of staff should also have objectives agreed and their performance assessed with local needs and the school improvement plan in mind' (McCormac, 2011: 54, Recommendation 4).

The importance of training to conduct professional reviews is also stressed in the McCormac recommendations: 'Staff acting as reviewers in the PRPD process should be properly trained and their involvement in the process should be seen as an important part of their own professional development' (McCormac, 2011: 54, Recommendation 5).

Perhaps the peer learning process itself could be seen as part of this training? Indeed, there are similar skills in both initiatives:

• the reflection on and articulation about one's practice

• the identification of strengths and development needs

• the concept of an action plan to target specific development.

Of course, the accountability agenda will not go away, but participants might feel more secure if they have already had practice in talking about their own performance and in identifying needs. Certainly, they would be more able to discuss plans for moving forward.

In the past, it may be true that once-a-year reviews floundered because they were seen as somehow separate from daily practice; as a formal opportunity to stop and suddenly reflect, with the added pressure of having to come up with a list of strengths and needs – and all of this often with someone you were unaccustomed to sharing such information with.

How much better then to have already had a number of constructive, supportive articulations with someone who had the role of facilitating your reflections? How much better if this formal annual review took the form of an overview of the many previous sessions where the agenda was self-generated and the reflections genuine and meaningful?

In their report, the Scottish Government suggest that: 'when planning CPD activities, teachers and their managers should consider the particular needs of the individual, whilst taking account of school, local and national priorities' (Donaldson, 2010: 62).

The needs of the individual are difficult to properly identify and discuss if they are only considered once a year in a review of progress. The professional review is about taking stock, evaluating performance and matching it against a standard, whereas peer learning is about personal reflections on day-to-day practice – shared in a professional context of non-judgemental discovery.

However, it is possible for peer learning to prepare the way, develop skills and confidence, and assemble some of the information and evidence that would make the review much more meaningful, more powerful and more authentic.

> There are increasing examples of professional learning communities which support and challenge one another around agreed areas for improvement. There is also some evidence that effective collegiate working has led to increased opportunities for teachers to be involved in decision-making and to lead aspects of school improvement. (Donaldson, 2010: 66)

Paper Trails

Although the initiatives outlined in this book are concerned with a peer learning interaction where the person reflecting establishes the agenda and has ownership of the planned next steps for development, it is still possible to build in some documented evidence of the process. It may be that a paper trail will be useful to look back on to monitor one's own professional development. It may be that management request some kind of evidence that the interaction has taken place and that there is a planned focus for the outcomes that have arisen from the meeting. It may be that management need some indication of development and the kind of support required to fully support staff – whether this be in terms of arranging formal CPD and staff development, or simply to provide the materials necessary to support a practitioner's initiative. Either way, we need to look at how the interaction can be supported and enhanced via some kind of record, without it dominating or deflecting us from genuine articulated reflections.

Below is detailed a possible pro forma used by a local primary school teacher to record his reflections. A blank template of this is available in Appendix 2. Readers might wish to adapt/modify it to suit their own context/stage of development.

Reflections of: Joe Soap	Supported by: Sandra M.
Date: October	Subject discussed: Farming project
Focus of discussion: Classroom display as feedback to pupils	
Joe discussed how he has been trying to provide effective feedback through his comments and stickers on the farming artwork. He realized that his comments might come across as a little negative and that pupils were becoming rather competitive about the number of 'stars' awarded. We discussed the difference between being successful because you have natural artistic talent and success because you work hard and learn through being diligent. Joe acknowledged that he should try to reward effort as much as raw talent.	
Planned next steps:	
Joe is going to establish a more equitable system and success criteria for his 'star' awards. He wants to involve pupils in peer assessment and to give credit more consistently to those who work hard and make personal progress rather than achieve good results because they are naturally talented. Work will receive feedback on a two stars and a wish basis with a more positive feel to it.	
What success will look like:	
Pupils will be more involved in establishing what constitutes 'progress'. More emphasis will be put on progress and fulfilling the success criteria than on producing 'good artwork'. There will be more focus on learning and developing in the feedback and general classroom dialogue.	
Evidence of success:	
The comments on the artwork with feedback from the pupils and from Joe. Discussing progress and 'good artwork' with the class collectively and individually.	
Next meeting planned for: November	

Figure 5.1

Clearly from the example above, we can see that Joe has been enabled to explore his approach towards feedback for the artwork in his class. He has been enabled to reflect on and consider his own values in terms of product over process and has concluded that there should be more emphasis on the effort and development of artistic skill than on raw talent alone. His reflections have been articulated and an action plan arrived at. His partner in the interaction has helped him to establish what success will look like and she will have the opportunity to discuss this further in their next meeting.

Into Action

Of course, documenting reflections are only part of the story. What is needed is some way of turning these reflections into action. The pro forma above provides opportunities for recording planned action for personal development. This might be something as simple as planning to keep on doing something that is working well, or as dramatic as an urgent request for some professional development session or course of training.

These peer learning interactions can enable someone to have very specific information about their practice. As the example above shows, Joe really wanted to think about the artwork and was helped to make changes to his own attitudes and values as well as to what he did in the classroom.

Such interactions and their documentation can lead the way to further development, or can provide evidence that reflection and development are indeed taking place. However, it is important that the exercise does not degenerate into a meaningless paper exercise for the benefit of someone else. The important thing here is that Joe realized something about himself and his practice. He worked out changes to make things better. The paper trail is a reminder for him and evidence to others that he does reflect, and that he is developing. The record of the interaction is a tool and just that – a record, not an extra piece of bureaucracy.

Later in the year, a professional looking back over a number of interactions, may be able to see patterns and themes emerging. It may be possible to clearly identify strengths and needs over a period of time – as opposed to the 'snapshot' view generally produced from a one-off inspection of practice, or through an annual look back at the year in general. To be able to look back at a record of the developing professional would be invaluable. To be able to represent yourself as someone who reflects often and then goes on to do something about it would also be very valuable, and very professional. Certainly, there can be a link between peer learning interactions and the annual PRD session, but such a meeting would be so much more informed with evidence like the pro forma example shown above as a focus for discussion.

Is There Another Way? Can We Integrate Some of These Approaches?

It is true that there are many ways of developing reflective practice. Each of the examples in this book has its own strategies, strengths and purposes. Although similar, these approaches do not detract from each other. It is unlikely that doing one means that you hinder another. Therefore, is it possible to use them together, as part of a continuum – moving from novice to expert; from beginning with a lot of support or structure, towards being an expert, with much to reflect upon? Is it possible then to establish a continuum from novice to expert? To provide a raft of experiences which, taken together, over time, will equip staff with the confidence, the skills and the experience to conduct these sessions?

Progression: A Raft of Approaches

The first chapter of this book looked at a range of approaches to reflective practice which are currently being used in schools across the UK and the rest of the world.

What is needed next is to see how some of these might be combined to provide a range of experiences to support and evidence reflective practice and professional development in school.

It is important to state that the lessons best remembered are those we learned for ourselves. Teachers realizing for themselves the areas for development will be more willing, more enlightened and more ready to make lasting changes to their practice than those who are merely responding to what others have told them. Indeed, many changes are resisted, consciously or otherwise, simply because someone else, usually in a position of power, is suggesting them.

Here is a combination of approaches designed to support and develop reflective practice in an institution. It moves from the personal, self-initiated, peer learning articulated, reflections through to more systematic, institution-wide approaches:

- Communities of practice

- Peer learning, no observation

- Peer learning, with observation

- Reflective evidence to inform development

- Other possible formats for recording reflections

- Lesson study

- Learning rounds

- Management observation

- Professional review and development

Communities of practice

The term 'communities of practice' was coined by Jean Lave and Etienne Wenger. It refers to the process of social learning that occurs when people have a common interest: 'Communities of practice are groups of people who share a concern or a passion for something they do and learn how to do it better as they interact regularly' (Wenger, 2006: 1).

The suggestion was that there was much to be learned incidentally through social interactions as long as certain conditions applied:

1 **The Domain:** there should be a group of people with a shared identity with a shared commitment.

2 **The Community:** in pursuit of their interests, the group engage in joint discussions and activities. They build relationships that enable them to learn from each other.

3 **The Practice:** they develop a shared repertoire of resources, experiences and practice. This takes time and sustained interaction.

These conditions are a fitting description of the experience in which students and emerging professionals find themselves. Certainly, the kind of peer learning interactions described in this book seem to be at one with these conditions. Wenger (2006) goes on to say: 'However, the very characteristics that make communities of practice a good fit for stewarding knowledge – autonomy, practitioner-orientation, informality, crossing boundaries – are also characteristics that make them a challenge for traditional hierarchical organizations.' (We will return to this issue and some of the challenges of developing reflection later on in this book.)

According to Wenger (2006):

> A growing number of associations, professional and otherwise, are seeking ways to focus on learning through reflection on practice. Their members are restless and their allegiance is fragile. They need to offer high-value learning activities. The peer-to-peer learning activities typical of communities of practice offer a complementary alternative to more traditional course offerings and publications.

Therefore, we will turn now to a raft of activities which might provide a development and structure incorporating both traditional and alternative approaches towards professional reflection.

Peer learning, no observation

A peer learning approach where the person doing the reflection talks, and their peer listens, *having not witnessed the lesson* seems a good place to begin. The fact that time and 'cover' do not need to be provided to facilitate some observation makes this a manageable and cost-effective approach. One benefit would be that the person doing the reflecting does not need to prepare a lesson especially to be observed. She does not need to feel any pressure about someone coming in to watch her teach. She should not feel threatened in any way that there are management agendas or judgemental issues going on. Another benefit is that there is no need to provide expensive cover for one class while the teacher goes to observe another.

To begin with this approach should help reluctant staff to open up the dialogue. Giving opportunities for staff to reflect on, articulate and explore their practice in this safe environment should help to develop confidence, build trust between peers and heighten the ethos of professionalism amongst the staff. This might be the first step in the development of a 'community of practice'. Even though it involves only two people, it still constitutes a community, as it fits the three characteristics discussed earlier: Domain, Community and Practice.

Peer learning, with observation

Moving on from this and developing practice further, staff could be invited to allow their peer learning partners to observe them teaching prior to the peer learning sessions. The session would still be structured so that the person doing the reflecting sets the agenda, the topic and does the articulation. However, the person who had observed the lesson might feel it appropriate to make more comments on the practice and next steps involved.

Sue, a student, tried the peer learning with and without observation and was able to see benefits in both approaches.

> In an observed lesson the person looking is looking with a critical eye, but not articulating their thoughts – so they are learning from that point of view. And then, in the interview afterwards, the person who was taking the lesson will, even though they might not need to describe as much as when the lesson wasn't observed, they will still learn as they reflect and articulate their thoughts.
>
> Because that person has seen it, you cannot hide from them. You cannot pretend that all went well if it didn't. It forces you into more honesty. You can't say it went really, really well, if it didn't. You have to face up to the fact that things didn't go well and that you had some disruption. You are made more accountable, but it's not like having a tutor there because there isn't that same pressure.
>
> You don't feel as bad if things go wrong or if there's been a mistake.
>
> Because you're learning together. It's not a power relationship. (Sue, PGDE student)

This sense of trust and partnership can lead quite naturally on to the next step where some kind of record of the interaction is kept. At this point, it may be appropriate to introduce some sort of record of the reflection.

Sue's partner in the interaction, Kelly, said:

> Sometimes there were long silences after Sue had spoken while I was trying to scribble things down, so then you get this extra silence where you're thinking, 'oh, maybe I should say something else'. So then you keep talking and then you do go deeper. You end up saying things that might have remained buried.
>
> It would be good to record it digitally so that the person reflecting could listen back and take time to think about it. You don't really hear it properly while you are reflecting, you're too busy thinking. We were making notes, but we couldn't get down everything. It would be really good to record it and listen again afterwards and use it as a listening exercise for yourself.

Reflective evidence to inform development

It is important that the staff involved feel some sort of 'ownership' of any accountability agenda. Ideally, staff would discuss and come up with a format for recording reflections. In this way, they would be more likely to have a shared understanding of the purpose, audience and format of the document to be created as part of the reflective process. For example, the bank of peer learning questions might provide something of a basis for recording professional reflections.

Again, the two students had something valuable to say about using one of the pro formas provided at the end of this book:

> Having a structure is better [than a blank sheet] because the person reflecting just has to think about their reflections, you almost don't even need to remember what you've been saying, because the person asking the questions is focused on making notes. They are also doing something; the person who is writing it down isn't reflecting on what the other person has to say because they are too busy doing the mechanics – so that takes the pressure off the other person.
>
> So it feels like more of your own flow of a monologue, as you say what you have in your head because the other person isn't so obviously 'fixed' on you. They're busy with their own job trying to get things down. (Kelly and Sue, PGDE students)

The kind of questions used to focus the articulations could be similar to those in the pro formas or those below:

Details of the lesson used for this reflection:

Why was this lesson chosen for reflection?

What did you want the pupils to learn?

What do you think they will remember?

What kind of thinking did you wish to promote?

How did you organize the lesson to be inclusive for all learners?

Were there any particular challenges or issues during the lesson?

Was there something you were particularly pleased with?

Was there any sense of frustration during the course of the lesson?

How might you do things differently another time?

It may then be useful to include a mini action plan or indication of how practice will be altered as a result of the reflection.

What will you do differently in terms of:

- planning and preparation?
- teaching and supporting?
- classroom management?
- rewards and sanctions, etc.?

How will you assess the impact of these changes on pupil learning?

What might your evidence be?

What will success/progress look like?

Such an approach might look like the one below, though this is by no means prescriptive. It would be much better if those involved included what they felt was most relevant and useful.

Other possible formats for recording reflections

Focus	Comment
Details of the context used for this reflection:	Drama lesson using mime to show emotions like fear and surprise.
Why was this context chosen for reflection?	Some pupils very self-conscious and unsure about how to use body language and facial expression to convey emotion.
What did you want the pupils to learn?	How to use body language and facial expression to convey emotion.
What do you think they will remember?	How their teacher modelled the miming of fear!
What kind of thinking did you wish to promote?	Empathy and consideration of how it might feel if you were very, very scared.
	Some thinking about how to evoke a response in the audience.
How did you organize the lesson to be inclusive for all learners?	We discussed emotion and how different people show it. We modelled some reactions. We discussed things that we find scary. I highlighted pupils who were able to mime the emotions well.
Were there any particular challenges or issues during the lesson?	J and P found it difficult to join in. They were inhibited and withdrawn.
Was there something you were particularly pleased with?	Most pupils were really engaged and entered into the spirit of things. G, M and B were especially good.
Was there any sense of frustration during the course of the lesson?	Yes, some pupils were rather silly and got quite carried away. Behaviour became an issue.

Focus	Comment
How might you do things differently another time?	I needed some signal for everyone to stop. Perhaps I shouldn't be so 'dramatic' myself!
	I need to support the pupils who were more inhibited and to 'manage' the more boisterous ones.
	See action plan for more details.
How will you assess the impact of these changes?	I will reflect on the next lesson in terms of the overall behaviour of the class and the involvement of the more inhibited pupils.
What might your evidence be?	More involvement from J and P. Peer feedback from the 'ability groups' that I will set up for the next lesson to support them.
What will success/ progress look like?	Class on task, well behaved and prepared to 'have a go' at the skills involved without feeling too shy and silly.
What did you learn about yourself/your practice from this reflection?	I think that I get a bit carried away with a 'good idea' sometimes. I was enjoying 'performing' too much and should have thought things through in more detail. I need to think about how the class might react and remember – it's about them, not me!
Action/plan for next steps:	• Organize groups in a way that supports the shy child. • Give roles to pupils in each group so we don't get the louder pupils dominating. • Think through the next plan and anticipate possible 'flash points' where I need to rein them in. • Introduce a signal for attention: try 'little bells'.

Figure 5.2

The teacher involved would then outline how they might do things differently in order to improve the situation.

The aim here is to introduce a low-key format for recording the reflections and the impact of the reflections on planning for teaching and learning. It may be that there will sometimes be little to record or change, and times where there is a lot to grapple with. However, given that the teachers themselves will decide which lesson/incident to discuss, it is likely that there will always be some point in discussing and analysing what happened and considering what it is that they feel is needed in order to move things along. It might help to promote confidence and trust if the written documents remain with the person whose reflections they represent: 'The other thing is that we didn't keep copies of the things that we wrote. The person taking notes gave those notes to the other person. It was their reflections. It was not about us, because we'd written it we just handed it over' (Kelly and Sue, PGDE students).

In many authorities, there are electronic portfolios of reflective practice, CPD learning, etc. It may be that the above framework could be adapted for such a record. Indeed, such a framework may well already exist. However, it would be best if staff involved felt that sense of ownership and understanding whilst still at this early stage of recording reflections.

Lesson study

A natural progression would be the inclusion of some version of the 'lesson study' approach. This approach would enable the partners to work together and to conduct observation and feedback with a definite focus on teaching and learning. It is an excellent way to introduce another professional into the classroom and provides a collaborative approach to developing practice. The teachers involved would look at an area of practice that they want to improve. Together, they plan some ideas to take things forward, then one of them teaches the lesson whilst the other observes. Later, the 'learning conversation' takes place, using a peer learning approach initially, before going on to make a more formal evaluation of practice linked to next steps. Ideally, the roles would be reversed for the next step in order for the observation and feedback roles to be shared. The skills and experiences gained in the peer learning sessions would support this approach well. Again, this is a further development of the communities of practice approach devised by Wenger (1998).

Learning rounds

Once staff have had some experience in being observed and doing the observations, it would be easier to introduce the 'learning rounds'. Initially, staff would be invited to volunteer to take part. Staff would meet to discuss the focus for observation. This might well be linked to or spring from the experiences in the 'lesson study' activities.

As discussed earlier, several members of staff would observe a lesson with a previously agreed focus. Later, they would meet to discuss what they had learned about learning and teaching in a professional, non-personal manner. Many schools would do this with no feedback at all to the teacher being observed, however it might be preferable to give some brief indicator of some of the strengths of the lesson.

As Wenger (2006) puts it: 'Communities develop their practice through a variety of methods, including: problem solving, requests for information, seeking the experiences of others, reusing assets, coordination and synergy, discussing developments, visiting other members, mapping knowledge and identifying gaps' (p.1).

Management observation

At some point in time, the school management team will need to make some developmental observations of lessons. In ITE, tutors will need to evaluate student performance. However, having moved through this raft of ideas the session could be so much more focused. The experience of having reflected often, having worked collegiately and taken part in observation and feedback approaches such as learning rounds, means that participants could go into discussions about their practice with knowledge and confidence. Moreover, if things did not go well on the day, they would have the information and evidence to present a much more accurate picture of themselves as professionals when the feedback interaction takes place.

Professional review and development

The same is of course true for professional review and development/ appraisal meetings. The experience and evidence collected over a number of peer learning interactions, together with the experiences outlined in this raft of approaches, means that any PRD session conducted can benefit from those involved having more experience, confidence and evidence to hold a much more equal and professional discussion regarding strengths and development needs. Such a grounding would contribute to a greater involvement and sense of ownership on the part of the person being reviewed, and give them the tools and information required to outline what they feel they need to do to develop professionally.

Summary

In this chapter, we considered different kinds of accountability and some of the advantages and disadvantages of them. We looked at how professionals might be made accountable currently and how paper trails might be created in order to track professional development. We considered some of the advantages and disadvantages of some of these approaches. There was a proposal for a raft of measures being introduced in order to

(Continued)

(Continued)

link current reflection approaches together in a developmental contin-uum supporting the novice professional on their journey to full capacity. There was discussion regarding communities of practice, and how they might be established in order to develop relationships between peers. The core characteristics of communities of practice form a fundamental structure for this, and this, in turn, facilitates the peer learning approach and the raft of reflective practices advocated in this chapter. Some ideas were then explored concerning paper trails for the structuring and recording of professional reflections and some ideas to support turning '*reflection* on practice' into '*action* on practice'.

Questions for Reflection

- Consider what you think about the raft of approaches. Does the sequence fit into your own context? Is there any benefit in missing some of these out?
- Think about how professionals might record their reflections. Try out a peer learning interaction using one of the pro formas to record your thoughts. You might need to adapt these to suit your own context and stage of development.
- Consider how a series of peer learning interactions might enable you to represent yourself more adequately when in a situation where you are being assessed on your abilities or when you are engaged in some review of your professional progress.
- Is there anything that you might need to do to enhance the sug-gestions outlined in this chapter?

Further Reading

- Nias, J. (1989) *Primary Teachers Talking: A Study of Teaching as Work*. London: Routledge, pp. 181–97.
- Smith, R. and Coldron, J. (1998) 'Thoughtful teaching', in A. Cashdan and L. Overall (eds) *Teaching in Primary Schools*. London: Cassell, pp. 63–7.
- Storey, A. and Hutchinson, S (2001) 'The meaning of teacher professionalism in a quality control era', in F. Banks and A. Shelton Mayes (eds) *Early Professional Development for Teachers*. London: David Fulton/The Open University.

References

Clutterbuck D. and Megginson D. (1999) *Mentoring Executives and Directors*. Oxford: Butterworth-Heinemann.

Donaldson, E. (2010) *Teaching Scotland's Future Report on the Review of Teacher Education in Scotland*. Edinburgh: The Scottish Government.

General Medical Council (GMC) (2009) *Tomorrow's Doctors: Outcomes and Standards for Undergraduate Medical Education.*

Ghaye, T. (2011) *Teaching and Learning Through Reflective Practice: A Practical Guide for Positive Action*. London: Routledge.

Kennedy, A. and Allan, J. (2009) '"The assessor and the assessed": learning from students' reflections on peer-evaluation', *Journal of Teacher Education and Teachers' Work*, 1(1).

McCormac, E. (2011) *Advancing Professionalism in Scottish Teaching: Report of the Review of Teacher Employment in Scotland*. Edinburgh: The Scottish Government.

Scottish Government (2004) *Guidance on the Procedure for Professional Review and Development for Teachers in Scotland*. Edinburgh: The Scottish Government.

Smith, R. and Coldron, J. (1998) 'Thoughtful teaching', in A. Cashdan and L. Overall (eds) *Teaching in Primary Schools*. London: Cassell, pp. 63–7.

Wenger, E. (1998) *Communities of Practice: Learning, Meaning, and Identity.* Cambridge: Cambridge University Press.

Wenger, E. (2006) *Communities of Practice: A Brief Introduction*. Available at: www. ewenger.com/theory

Wildman, T. and Niles, J. (1987) 'Reflective teachers: tensions between abstractions and realities', *Journal of Teacher Education*, 3: 25–31.

What do teachers and students think of 'peer learning interactions'?

Chapter Overview

In this chapter, we will look at how peer learning interaction has been received and how students perceive the process as part of their continuous professional development. This approach has been used for both the post-graduate and Bachelor of Education courses since 2009. Some research into student perceptions was done in 2010 and this chapter will look at some of the findings and their implications.

• The aim of the peer learning interactions research
• Methodology
• Case study 1: Heather
• Case study 2: Teresa
• Case study 3: Darren

For a few years now, we have been using peer learning interactions as a major plank in our support of student teachers at the University of Edinburgh. Nearly a thousand students have been introduced to reflective practice through this approach. Students are introduced to the approach early in the programme and then are encouraged to pair up with another student who is on placement in another school. Through each placement, they hold peer learning interactions and record something of 'what they learn' in their professional development portfolio, which they refer to later in consultation with a university tutor.

The Aim of the Peer Learning Interactions Research

At the University of Edinburgh, students were asked to take part in peer learning interactions whilst out on placement in schools. These interactions were then followed up with questionnaires inviting them to reflect on the experience. Some students were later followed up for interviews to provide further feedback, and some of these interviews feature in the case studies elsewhere in this book.

The focus for the research involved asking students how effective the peer learning approach was in terms of developing a reflective approach to teaching.

The project was introduced and supported through a series of lectures and workshops broadly following the development approach set out in Chapter 4.

Key principles of the approach were supported by the work of Ghaye and Ghaye (1998: 16–18). Reflective practice seen as discourse involves:

- a reflective turn – looking also at the ordinary and routine

- learning how to account for ourselves – to describe, explain and justify our teaching

- a disposition to enquiry – to develop the ability to question, to systematically and continuously strive to learn

- a social constructivist approach to learning.

Methodology

Students were given questionnaires to complete to gather data on their experiences with the peer learning approach. These questionnaires set out to investigate their level of confidence in their ability to reflect in a meaningful way about their teaching experiences. This was supported by interviews with a focus group of students, to look in more detail at their experiences. Comments from their mid-placement review statements were also used to explore evidence of the impact of this approach.

The Survey

In the survey, there were nine questions.

Question 1: What were the benefits of the peer learning experience for you?

Students were asked to select from a list of *possible benefits of the experience:*

		Agree or strongly agree
1	Support from someone in the same situation	93
2	Good to have another viewpoint	93
3	Someone who understood the workload and time restrictions	88
4	Someone in a different context to compare/share ideas with	86
5	Someone to listen	85
6	Chance to observe and express my reflections	83
7	Someone non-judgemental	81
8	A break from the stress of the placement	64
9	Helped me to feel less isolated	60

Figure 6.1

Student Responses

It was really good to share experiences and helped me reflect on how I was progressing on placement. As placement was so busy, it was nice to have specific time to talk about it with someone who knows what you're going through!

Describing how I taught a lesson was beneficial as it gave me time to review how I could have approached it differently. (4th Year BEd Primary, 2010)

I feel the benefits of the peer learning experience for me was just getting the chance to share ideas, successes and difficulties we had found along the way. It made me feel a lot more confident that others were having the same kind of experiences as myself and we could support each other to help us both develop our skills. Definitely worthwhile. (4th Year BEd Primary)

I enjoyed being able to discuss the lesson in particular and my progress in general with someone who is going through the same thing at the same time. It definitely feels less judgemental than discussing things with the class teacher or university tutor. I was able to gain insights and suggestions from my peer partner that I may not have thought of myself. It was great to be able to share good ideas and successful technique and practice. (4th Year BEd Primary)

Commentary

These responses indicate that the students really appreciated having someone there who understood their situation and workload, and someone who was able to provide another viewpoint. In total 83 per cent appreciated having the chance to express their reflections out loud, with 81 per cent appreciating having had someone non-judgemental to listen to them. This is significant in terms of the notion of learning being socially constructed. It echoes the comments earlier in this book about the importance of actually articulating our reflections in order to fully acknowledge them. A sense of professional reflection and the freedom to explore practice come through the student comments above. Palmer considers this social interaction as being vital to creating a supportive 'learning community':

We need ways to listen more openly to each other; to judge and advise and 'fix' each other much less; to find the strengths – not just the weaknesses – in each others' proposals; to leave each other feeling heard and affirmed as well as stretched and challenged when our conversations ends. (Palmer, 1993: 11)

The Survey

Question 2: What were the challenges of the peer learning experience for you?

Students were asked to select from a list of possible challenges involved in engaging with peer learning interactions whilst on placement:

		Agree or strongly agree	Disagree or strongly disagree
1	Finding time to visit	87	9
2	Finding time to arrange the meeting	75	15
3	Creating an action plan to follow up the meeting	63	15
4	Remaining professional in the discussion	45	35
5	Writing up what I learned in my folder	41	42
6	Being a facilitator and not an advisor	32	36
7	Convincing the school of its value	26	59
8	Asking too many questions	23	47

Figure 6.2

Commentary

The major issue for ITE students was that of time. Finding time in a short, busy placement was seen as a considerable challenge. One factor here was the fact that they had to arrange to go to another school to observe a lesson and then have the peer learning interaction. This took some of them around three hours. Then of course there would be the reciprocal visit taking up another three hours. There was the suggestion that it would be better for students to be paired up in the same school in order to allow more time. However, doing so would mean that the students would not see a different school, a different context, a different way of operating. Of course, having peer learning interactions without the element of observation would certainly save time and make the process more manageable, however students did appreciate all of the benefits of seeing another context and seeing teaching done by a peer at the same stage of development. The other major finding was the challenge they found in recording the interaction and turning the professional articulation into professional action. At the time of the study, the students did not have the benefit of some of the resources provided in this book. In Chapter 5, there are some pro formas for recording reflections and for structuring the move from reflection into action. In future interactions, it is hoped that these will provide some support to the challenges identified in the survey.

Student Responses

It was really useful to be able to see another school and classroom environment and to speak to other pupils and teachers. My partner's school was so much different from mine and it really opened my eyes to how a different situation can throw up so many different challenges.

I found it very beneficial to observe another student who is at the same level as me as it gave me an idea of my progress and also strategies I could use in the classroom. It also opened up the opportunity to gain an experience of another school even though I was not placed there. The school I was at was very different from my peer tutor's and this enabled us to compare experiences really well.

I found the peer learning experience very useful and beneficial for my own professional development. I liked going into a different school and seeing a completely new classroom with different ways of working. (4th Year BEd Primary student)

Commentary

Another consideration is the challenge of keeping things formal and sticking to the approach where one person facilitates for the other to do the articulation and the 'working it out for themselves'. Students who had not been in touch throughout the placement period said that there was a huge temptation to use the time for a 'catch-up', which was both professional and personal, and perhaps this distracted them from the purpose of the interactions.

Student Responses

I thought the question bank was useful because it stopped us from talking about irrelevant stuff and kept the conversation professional. (4th Year BEd Primary student)

For some participants, it was the notion of performing in front of a friend that made them nervous.

I didn't know her so well really, so I was feeling pretty nervous at the idea of her coming in to see my lesson. I know she would be ok but still it was a bit nerve racking. (4th Year BEd Primary student)

Commentary

Certainly, this is significant and suggests that if observation is to be part of the process there should be opportunities for the participants to develop the kind of trust and professional relationship that will reassure them. However, as suggested elsewhere in this book, the approach where the other person does not observe the lesson has much to offer, as it gets over this sense of nerves and apprehension, and it might be an early step which later on leads to lessons which include observation. However, not every student felt this way and it is important to remember that in teaching, as in many professions, being observed is very much a part of day-to-day practice.

Student Responses

> I found that the peer learning experience was very useful for my development as a teacher. It was interesting to see how other schools operated and the different methods of behaviour management and reward systems. It was nice to be able to watch someone else teach then share your experiences or even to give them advice. It was a confidence boost.

These comments reinforce the notion that getting away from any controlling agendas and moving towards a peer interaction was beneficial for these students.

> Barriers of power and difference are assumed to be reduced when peers speak with each other, compared to when students and teachers interact. In these circumstances more open communication can therefore occur, allowing for fuller engagement and potentially greater opportunities for learning (as distinct from teaching). This can be seen as one important move to disperse and horizontalise pedagogical power and authority. (Boud and Lee, 2005: 501–16)

The Survey

Students were provided with a question bank to structure their peer learning sessions (see Chapter 5 and also the appendix).

> This approach does not let you wander around hoping that you will bump into something that makes sense, but focuses attention on professional values, practice, improvement and context. (Ghaye and Ghaye, 1998 preface)

> It is however just as important to use the reflective conversation to enable the teller to focus upon those aspects of their teaching that are going well, to articulate the reasons for this and to construct action play to nourish and sustain the good things. (Ghaye and Ghaye, 1998: 21)

Question 3: How useful was the question bank?

It was invaluable	3.6%
It was very helpful	44%
It provided a good start	47%
It wasn't very useful	1.8%
I did not use it	3.6%

Figure 6.3

Student Responses

The question bank was very useful as it kept you focused, on task and didn't create the added worry of what should I be looking for or at.

It was a great starting point for then creating some of your own questions.

It also encouraged us to look at the same things for each of our individual lessons.

It was good because the question bank covered everything that a tutor would. (4th year BEd Primary students)

Commentary

There was a very positive response to this question. Over 94 per cent of the students felt that the question bank helped them to stay focused and remain professional. Almost half of the respondents saw it as a good start for professional reflection. It is important to acknowledge, however, that it is the articulation of these reflections, the manner in which the questions are asked, and the ethos in which the interactions take place that provide the basis for developing reflection in this way.

The question bank was well used and very much appreciated by students. It provided a clear structure *and* enabled them to focus on learning rather than getting side-tracked into anecdotal chatter. A high percentage of them felt that it kept things professional and reflective.

When possibility is present, people focus on what they want to create, not what they want to avoid. What they want more of, not less of. They welcome new ideas, see challenges and opportunities, and discuss and respect differences without attacking people. (Ghaye, 2011: 49)

It seems that having such a structure of reflective questions, whatever the profession, as a focus is beneficial. Once the kind of question is internalized, then the formal list of questions can perhaps be discarded.

The Survey

In the next question, students were asked about the point of reflecting.

Question 4: What is the point in having the question bank to structure interactions?

Student Responses

I think the question bank was a good focus point as the task may have turned more into a conversation talking about what happened rather than a learning conversation thinking of next steps etc. (4th Year BEd Primary student)

It helps to keep things reflective and professional	24%
It helps to structure the conversation	44%
It provided a good start	31%
It provided all we needed to reflect well	0%
It was not necessary	1%
It was a distraction	0%

Figure 6.4

Commentary

Again, we see here the significance of providing a structure for the interactions: 68 per cent of the students saw the question bank as a way of structuring the interaction and keeping it professional. A word of caution here is that the question bank should not be used as a systematic list, or as a tick-box exercise, dwelling equally and sequentially on each and every question. Instead, it should be seen as a framework, a menu of possible questions to support and facilitate interactions. It would be better to ask only one question, if that is all it takes to enable the other person to begin to reflect, articulate and develop understanding of their practice. However, at the early stages of professional reflection the question bank clearly provides a useful service. In time, the questions will be internalized and the person facilitating will be better able to 'go with the flow' of the person reflecting in as unobtrusive a manner as possible.

> 'Reflective conversations that are empowering enable the teachers to name, define and construct their own "realities"; they enable the teacher to sustain themselves. They nourish their sense of professional dignity.' (Ghaye and Ghaye, 1998: 23)

There are many benefits beyond the 'product' of reflection. It is important to see the professional value of reflection. It increases self-confidence and self-awareness, develops a range of skills and ultimately can help us to shape our values and professional attitudes.

The Survey

Question 5: Is it important to know the other person well?

Commentary

For students in Initial Teacher Education, the significance of knowing the other person doing the reflecting is evident: 74 per cent felt that it was helpful. Considering the stage of their professional development and their levels of anxiety, this is hardly surprising. However, what is perhaps more surprising is the fact that 20 per cent felt that it didn't really matter. This suggests that, for some at least, the ethos of trust where another person enables you to articulate your reflections free from a sense of judgement is, in fact, more significant than the relational elements of the experience. This reflection on the experience is indeed very professional. It gets right at the heart of the notion of a 'professional monologue', where the reflection and the learning come from the person reflecting, and not from the advice (offered or imposed) of another.

It is essential to know the other person well	4%
It helps if you know the other person well	70%
It doesn't matter if you don't know the other person well	20%
It is an advantage if you don't know the other person well	6%

Figure 6.5

Student comment

It was quite nice that I had time to talk and to figure things out myself.

She made me think about how to apply things to other lessons, she didn't just tell me, she made me think. (4th Year BEd Primary student)

Question 6: Is it important to see the other person teach?

It is essential to see the other person teach	41%
It helps if you see the other person teach	52%
It doesn't matter if you don't see the other person teach	7%
It is an advantage if you don't see the other person teach	0%

Figure 6.6

Commentary

The value of seeing someone else teach was very much appreciated. This opportunity to see someone else who is at the same point on the learning journey is very valuable. 'Many people like to reflect alone and calmly analyse the facts of the situation, without allowing emotion to cloud their judgement. Some people find that it helps to write things down… others recognize the benefits of talking things through, either with those who have been directly involved in the issue or with someone more impartial.' (Ghaye, 2011: 79)

Clearly for students at this stage in their learning, it is important for them to gain as wide a range of experience as possible. Seeing inside different establishments, seeing different organizational structures and seeing different professionals at work are essential for providing a well-balanced view of what the profession is all about. One of the benefits of the experience for the students in this survey was having the opportunity to visit another school and see how things were done elsewhere. However, this could just as easily have happened without them having to observe another student teach. Indeed, widening the range of student experiences might be best achieved outside of a peer learning initiative.

Having someone else in the classroom is something that early professionals (and many experienced ones!) still find rather intimidating. Perhaps an approach is needed where there is a balance, with one interaction following an *observed lesson,* and another conducted *without observation*. This might provide a 'best of both worlds' approach to structure and developing reflection for emerging professionals.

Student Responses

I found the peer learning experience beneficial in that it gave me the opportunity to receive feedback on my teaching from someone who is in exactly the same position that I am, and who I respect. I found delivering the observed lesson and the feedback session was much more relaxed than those with the university tutor as I did not feel that I was being 'judged' or scored.

It was good that you observed someone at the same level as you teach and get feedback from them too. It felt less formal and less stressful than a tutor visit. I felt that my peer tutor was there to help and support me rather than pick up on the negative points. It was constructive criticism.

It was nice to be able to watch someone else teach then share your experiences. It was a confidence boost.

I feel me and my partner had a successful learning conversation and I came away from it with new ideas and I felt confident about using these. I feel that we worked together to solve the problems we were encountering by discussion and reflection, coming up with a solution which we were able to try out when we got back to the classroom.

It made me feel less isolated and was comforting to know that someone with the same pressures, workload and stress levels took the time to visit and provide feedback. I feel the benefit of the peer learning experience for me was just getting the chance to share ideas, successes and difficulties we had found along the way.

It is a good time to make mistakes and learn from them. To have feedback from one of my peers helped me to become aware of where my strengths/weaknesses were. I was reflecting on what I could have done better and what I needed to further practise in my teaching skills before the tutor visit and I think that I gained a little more confidence by the time she came out to see me.

It made me feel a lot more confident that others were having the same kind of experiences as myself and we could support each other to help us both develop our skills. It was definitely worthwhile.

I felt that peer learning really gave me an opportunity to work in conjunction with someone else who was in the same situation as I was. It was comforting to know at times that there may be difficulties that arise throughout placement, however the 'peer partner' actually doubled up as a 'peer supporter'. (4th Year BEd Primary students)

 Case study 1: Heather Lucas, PGDE student

What was the difference between peer learning conversations with someone you had seen teach/had seen you teach and someone who had not?

The main difference that I found between doing a peer learning conversation with someone who had seen me teach and someone who had not was that when the person had not seen me teach I had to describe and analyse in much greater detail what went on. I was not able to make any assumptions about the other person already knowing something. When I had a conversation with the person who had seen me teaching I left a lot out about my lesson because she had seen it for herself and therefore I felt it was irrelevant to our conversation. However in having a conversation with someone who did not see me teach I realized the significance of those things I had previously left out and how beneficial the discussion of them was to me and my partner.

Were there any advantages/disadvantages?

Advantages: allowed the opportunity to be more self-critical and look further into what my teaching entailed.

Did you use different skills?

When the other person has not seen you teach you have to be much more descriptive and analytical as well as critical.

Which approach enabled you/your partner to be more reflective and analytical?

I believe that not having seen each other teach enabled us to be much more reflective and analytical. It gave us the opportunity to break down

(Continued)

(Continued)

everything we did and explore what was good and what we could have improved on completely self-reflectively rather than thinking about what the other person would say. As well when the other person hadn't seen me teach, their questions were not catered to their opinion on the lesson but allowed me to truly think about what had happened and be prepared to answer any of the questions.

Any other comments about the process?

I feel that having a peer learning conversation with someone who has not seen me teach gives me the opportunity to be completely honest and critical about my teaching in the end providing a more valuable learning experience for both the people involved.

Clearly, Heather had a very positive experience with her peer. She did not allow the fact that she had not been observed get in the way of her reflections. Indeed, she positively thrived on the experience and was able to reflect positively on the experience afterwards. Many of the reasons she provides as benefits come across very persuasively. However, it might not be the best approach for everyone. ITE students also need to have opportunities to see other practitioners and other learning contexts. They can get these from visiting other schools. It is true that they could get this broader experience simply by visiting and not necessarily observing others teach. Yet probably the best scenario would be to do both: have an observational visit and peer learning interaction, and then meet up again and have an interaction which is not based on observation. In that way, they would get the benefit of both approaches.

The Survey

Question 7: Indicate, from a list provided, any of the skills you have developed in connection with the peer learning interactions

		Agree or Strongly agree	Disagree or Strongly Disagree
1	Reflecting	93	2
2	Actively listening	85	2
3	Giving feedback	85	4
4	Asking questions	81	4
5	Making suggestions	75	8
6	Summarising	70	6
7	Offering guidance	62	11
8	Advising	58	13
9	Paraphrasing	51	8

Figure 6.7

Student Responses

My peer supporter helped me realize this was a learning process.

She kept eye contact with me and made me feel she was really listening.

My supporter was really positive and encouraging.

My supporter didn't just ask a question for the sake of it, he was genuinely interested in what I had to say.

They listened to me, really listened and that doesn't happen everywhere.

They stayed quiet long enough to let me expand on it.

She ignored the script and let me talk, used only four key questions and they worked.

She made me feel important.

(4th Year BEd Primary students)

Commentary

There is a clear link here to the skills introduced in preparing for the interactions. The reflection, questioning and active listening are essential skills for effective professional reflection. However, the high percentage of responses indicating that 'giving feedback' was a skill that the students developed, suggests that the interactions were not purely situations where a professional monologue was taking place.

Many students felt the need to move from the initial, facilitator role, to one of a co-constructor of understanding, of a joint problem- solver. For students at this point in their learning, this is both inevitable and desirable. One of the benefits of the approach is that the partners do not feel pressured or judged. The participants should feel free to explore their practice and to plan ideas and strategies which will support and develop their practice. Experiments, which arise on the basis of their discussion, should be possible without the fear of censure or failure. Therefore at this stage, the 'two-way' reflection is beneficial. Later on, as they become more experienced at reflecting and at teaching, there will be less need for 'advice' and more opportunity for developing personal reflection and for 'finding out for oneself'. It is important to allow for this development from reflection into action. Once the reflection moves into the 'so what will I do next', it should be flexible enough to permit a joint enterprise where the participants problem-solve and come up with ideas. However, there is a difference between going through an articulation process and arriving at a place where professionals can jointly (and free from a sense of judgement) create possible solutions, and a situation where one person announces judgement and imposes a solution on what they perceive to be the problem.

> As we listen to others speak about their teaching we are free to say an inward, 'yes' to things that sound like us, and 'no' to the things that do not. We are free to speak about our own practice in a way that makes us only as vulnerable as we choose to be – a freedom that makes the conversation both possible and fruitful. We can explore our own identities in relation to other teachers' without ever feeling that we are being told to do our work in someone else's way. (Palmer, 1993)

If the result of the interaction is a decision to work together for a plan that will support professional development, this is a much more productive and professional approach. For students, it is an essential ingredient for continuous professional development. Palmer's suggestion that we can explore our own identities is particularly relevant here. Through the interaction, we can measure how 'like us' it is and explore what we might do to continue to do well, what we do well, and to improve on parts that need to be improved. Through this kind of focused professional dialogue, we can begin to form our professional identity and understand some of our professional values.

> 'We need ways to listen more openly to each other: to judge and advice and "fix" each other much less; to find the strengths not just the weaknesses – in each other's proposals; to leave each other feeling heard and affirmed as well as stretched and challenged when our conversations end' (Palmer, 1993: 11).

The Survey

Question 8: Consider some different approaches to support whilst on placement

Student Responses

Learning Interaction with a tutor only	3%
Peer Learning Interaction with a peer only	2%
Tutor observation and feedback only	7%
Peer Learning Interaction and tutor observation and feedback	74%
Peer Learning Interaction plus Learning Interaction with a tutor	14%

Figure 6.8

Commentary

- Given different approaches to the placement, 93 per cent preferred an option *which included* some kind of peer learning opportunity.

- Only 7 per cent preferred the traditional tutor observation and feedback model.

- Peer learning followed by a tutor observation and feedback was the most popular option with 73 per cent.

Student Responses

The tutors can be very supportive.

They can give you advice on your lessons and help on how to improve them.

They give you their opinions from a professional point of view.

Tutor judgements are a snapshot of your time there. Although teaching files are available you may not perform at your best on the day of their visit and therefore be misjudged.

Although very valuable, receiving criticisms can knock your confidence.

It can be a bit nerve-racking!

As it is only for a short time you can feel the pressure to 'perform' instead of relaxing into teaching.

The tutor will not know the pupils in detail so may not completely understand any special requirements or complications.

It's really scary being observed where you know that you are being assessed.

You are only assessed on a forty minute period and nerves can make you act differently to the way you would normally teach.

You only meet once before placement and don't really keep in touch throughout unless there is a problem.

Some of the tutors may have different expectations.

It can cause anxiety and this can have a knock-on effect on your teaching.

Having a tutor in class can make you very nervous.

Nerves may make me a little more likely to make mistakes.

It can unsettle the children, having someone else in the class.

(4th Year BEd Primary students)

It is clear that for the students in the study some kind of peer learning interaction was very much appreciated as a way of structuring and developing reflective practice. Although some felt that they really needed the professional advice that comes from the more experienced tutor or teacher, they saw peer learning interactions as supportive and beneficial. It seems clear that the experience had a beneficial impact on student confidence and that the students felt the experience 'set them up' in some way for the more formal interaction of the tutor visit. This 'combination approach', where a raft of measures are put in place to support and develop reflective practice, is discussed more fully in Chapter 5. It is interesting to note that the more traditional, tutor observation visit and feedback model was preferred by only 7 per cent of the cohort – a sign that the many changes in ITE are long overdue, perhaps.

Student comments about Peer Learning Interactions

Question 9: Indicate what you feel about the peer learning interactions

Student Responses

> It was good that you observed someone at the same level as you teach and get feedback from them too. It felt less formal and less stressful than a tutor visit. I felt that my peer tutor was there to help and support me rather than pick up on all the negative points. It was constructive.

> I feel that a peer observing me is less formal than a tutor observation therefore think it is a valuable experience to allow you to prepare, build confidence and receive constructive criticism that will improve your teaching. It will also be useful to observe how a fellow teaches, as we have never before had this opportunity. (4thYear BEd Primary students)

Commentary

It is interesting to see how much the notion of a 'less formal' interaction is valued by the students. There is something about the mutual experience of two professionals at the same stage of development that enables them to work together in a non-judgemental way. Students felt that their own confidence developed as a result of these interactions and that they were positive learning experiences rather than situations leading to negative criticisms of their emerging practice.

Some general quotes from this cohort:

> I'm looking forward to the next experience and think it would be good to visit my peer more than once.

> I think this was a very beneficial experience personally and professionally and should be used in all placements where possible.

> I would definitely take part in peer tutoring again as I felt it was a really worthwhile activity to participate in.

> I think we can learn so much more from other students, as when we watch experienced teachers, they make it all look so much easier. My partner seemed much more 'like me', and together we felt that we could move on at our own pace.

On the face of it, the response was very positive, yet there is still a lot of work to do. The peer learning approach to reflection still needs students and teachers to be committed to the process. Time still needs to be found. The initiative still needs to be led. In ITE this is fairly straightforward as it is a prerequisite for the course. However, if you are not on the course, then it is essential that there is someone supporting and encouraging you to do this and not allow the act of reflection to fall to the bottom of the pile of things that you 'ought to do but never quite get around to'.

 ## Case studies 2 and 3: Teresa and Darren

Background to study

Having proved successful in Initial Teacher Education, it was important to consider peer learning interactions and continuous professional development. For the approach to be effective, it needed to work just as well with experienced professionals as with those at the start of their professional career.

Two teachers were approached and asked if they would be willing to have a 'conversation' about their practice. They were given a list of the focus questions and asked to be ready to talk about a lesson that they had taught recently that was significant to them in some way. They were also asked if they would allow this interaction to be filmed for educational purposes. There was, significantly, no observation included as part of this exercise.

The result of the video provides an excellent resource for introducing the approach to others. Both teachers provide evidence of reflection. They each, in their own way, realize something about their practice and then go on to plan action to make things better next time.

Case study 2: Teresa Reid, primary school teacher

Teresa had been teaching for around 10 years and was responsible for a Primary 6 class (9- and 10-year-olds). The focus questions used to encourage her to articulate her reflections are shown in bold below.

Do you think you learned anything about yourself as a teacher in this lesson?

I think I was expecting an awful lot, in a very short amount of time. I should have, with hindsight, made the lesson into two lessons. I do feel that there was so much expected of the pupils. At the end of it, although I wanted a metaphor poem, I'd had to teach them all about similes as well. I should have thought more carefully about the timing and about how I could have split it into two lessons. And I think also, my questioning on the day, I could have probed deeper, to extend it and challenge them more.

Is there any way you could have organized your lesson differently?

I could have organized it better, I could have split the groups so one had an activity to do so I had chance to work with the other group, and then extend them.

But you knew that when you planned the lesson and you chose not to, why was that?

Because in writing lessons I do like to keep them together, because we share our ideas, and I do think it's important that the lower ability and the more able work together to share ideas. I wanted them all to benefit from the whole class discussion. However I realize now that some of them needed a lot more support and I wish that I had built in an opportunity to also give them more focused support at the time. I suppose this is part of learning to know your class and what they are capable of as much as anything else.

Teresa was then asked some questions about the peer learning interaction itself. This meta-cognition was essential if she was going to appreciate just how the process of reflection can have a positive effect on her professional practice.

How did you find the questions in this interaction?

I think the first few questions were fine because these are the kinds of questions you ask yourself every day, before you plan a lesson, even during a lesson sometimes you're thinking, 'Are they getting this?' 'Do I need to change things?' So those questions I was quite happy with. It was when you probed a bit deeper. Delving deeper into why I was doing things and what I wanted from it, I was a bit like 'hmm, I'm going to have to sit and think a bit harder about this!' Because, although I do it on a daily basis, I don't usually have to explain myself. So I did think, 'Hmm! I'm going to have to think carefully about this.'

Why do teachers not do this?

They do 'do it', but they don't necessarily have the time and opportunities to do it in as much depth as possible. And I think, somebody actually asking the questions makes the difference. When it's you asking yourself the questions, you don't necessarily need to answer the questions there and then. Or you can choose not to and you can choose whenever you want, whereas when you're with someone else, you need to come up with an answer.

Is there any advantage/disadvantage in not having someone see the lesson?

It's better, for me I feel a lot better talking about it because I know that maybe the 'niggly' behaviour that went on hadn't been picked up by someone else, or maybe if I'd forgotten a resource and it hadn't been picked up. Whereas I can think about what the perfect lesson might have been like and still add in the problems I found.

So, you can have a conversation that focuses on the learning and what you learned about teaching and learning, and not get bogged down in some of the other issues?

Yes, I think that, when you're talking to your peers and it's anecdotal that's when you go into the behaviour, that's the anecdotal stories, 'oh so and so did this', and that's when you come away thinking, did we talk about the learning process or about the teaching process at all?

It's nice to be able to talk about this. And it's nice to be able to talk when nobody's interrupting you and you can say what you want to say about a lesson, and if there's something in particular that you feel good about you don't feel silly about it. In the staffroom you don't particularly want to say, 'Oh it's great they're all using metaphors in their writing now!'

It would be particularly good for someone like me and a primary one teacher because we deal with different things every day, but it's the same learning process and we could learn so much from each other in that sense.

(Continued)

(Continued)

You're obviously not talking about content here, so what is it?

Well, even though it's a different stage, it's the way they introduce a topic, or the way she got the pupils to present things, and I think, my goodness, I could do that with primary seven. There's no difference, I would just have to extend it slightly content wise, but actually, that strategy she used is one that I could use myself.

The very presence of having someone in your room might change the dynamic in the classroom, whereas having a ten minute conversation at the end of the day might be feasible.

Do you think teachers would find it difficult to discipline themselves to have this kind of a conversation?

I think it would need the focus questions, and it would take some time to get used to but I think it is very beneficial.

Clearly, Teresa benefited from the interaction. In some ways, she was able to be more reflective, more focused and more analytical due to her teaching experience. This level of reflection provides a depth of understanding that demonstrates her understanding of her practice and of her as a professional. Novice professionals might not get close to this without practice in reflection and experience in their chosen profession.

Case study 3: Darren Swan, primary school teacher

Darren had been teaching for around 10 years and was responsible for a Primary 7 class (10- and 11-year-olds). He was asked about the peer learning interaction and how he had found the experience of reflecting in detail on his practice.

It's been interesting for me and very useful. I can't remember the last time that I looked at a lesson in so much depth. I think I will really benefit from taking a lesson apart and really being honest with myself about the strengths and weaknesses of that lesson.

What did you learn?

As we've been speaking I've just realized myself that I've been a little bit mixed up with the success criteria for my lesson – I realized that I hadn't a clear enough idea of what the aim of the lesson was. I realized that I was maybe trying to cover too many things, perhaps I should have just stuck to one.

I think if I hadn't sat down with you just now and had this discussion with you, you know, that wouldn't have come to me.

You say it's not often you get to have this kind of conversation. What could be done to make that different?

You could maybe have a buddy system in school where you could sit down with a member of staff and reflect on lessons, you could maybe have a rota system so different teachers from different stages reflect on their lessons. I don't think you need long, maybe 5–10 minutes.

Is there an advantage or a disadvantage in the fact that I didn't see the lesson that you taught?

Interestingly, I think that, because you never saw the lesson it's very difficult for you to be judgemental. Therefore I think that as an individual I think that takes a lot of the pressure off.

Whereas, if you had seen the lesson I might feel as though your questions were a bit loaded. I might have felt a little bit more vulnerable and hesitant about opening up really about the lesson. I think that because you've not seen it, in some strange way I feel as though I can be really almost 100 per cent open and honest about it.

Do you feel that I've given you any advice?

Long pause:

I think, in a strange way, through making me reflect on my own lessons it's almost like you empowered me to give myself advice. I don't think you've given me any direct advice yourself, but because you've, because the way your questions have been structured, you know it's actually allowed me to reflect on the lesson and think of ways to improve.

So yes, I definitely think, in a round about way there's been advice given, but it's almost as if you've allowed me to give it to myself.

(Continued)

(Continued)

And it's much easier to take the advice you give yourself than when it's given to you by someone else?

Yes, yes, definitely! I think when someone else is giving you advice you quite often leave the meeting you know, with the negative aspects of it, not necessarily how you're going to improve. You're just left with the message, ah! that part of the lesson wasn't any good. Whereas this way, when we're actually talking it through you're left with how are you going to improve it, and surely that's the most important thing.

So how difficult do you think it would be for you to do what I've been doing?

I feel as though I've benefited from it and been given advice, but as I say you've not actually given advice.

I think if I had the right toolkit of questions, if I had some guidance of how to go about conducting the interview, the discussion, then I would be able to do it with practice.

It was enjoyable. I don't often get time to reflect on an individual lesson and I think as long as you can trust each other, and also know that it's private as well and that you can properly open up and discuss your weaknesses as a teacher and think of ways that you can improve.

Maybe this is something where you need to build a relationship with somebody where you have that mutual trust.

If you were having a meeting like this with the management you would tend to err on the side of caution. I would be thinking certainly about the more positive aspects of the lesson without necessarily being fully honest about weaknesses and areas for improvement.

Doing it with someone from a different stage in the school might be interesting in terms of how different people reflect and the different strategies that they use not just in teaching but also in the ways they go about reflecting.

There might be some aspect of my own lesson that I've not even thought about and when I hear them reflecting on their own lesson it might encourage me to start thinking about that for myself.

If it was going to turn into a conversation with 50/50 people contributing their own ideas then it's not going to, necessarily, allow the teacher being interviewed to fully reflect on the lesson. I think you've allowed me to have much more of a flow.

It has been a bit of a monologue, but that has allowed me to reflect with much more detail about my lesson. Whereas if we're having a discussion, a conversation where you are discussing your lesson as well, I think it would have changed the focus a little bit.

If the person asking the questions knows that they are going to get an opportunity as well then it might be easier for them to just hold on.

I didn't want too many details about your lesson. I wasn't really interested in your lesson, I was interested in you and what you learn about your own practice. In that sense, it's different from a conversation. When you're in the position of asking the questions, you almost need to get into the zone, where you're hearing what the person is saying, but you're focusing on certain things, and the certain things are individual really, and the lesson itself doesn't matter – it's what you learn about that lesson.

Yes, that's right. It felt like it was my ideas, my lesson and my learning about myself as a teacher. It felt good!

Commentary

Again, the reflections of an experienced practitioner demonstrate a clear understanding of practice and the courage to reflect honestly about how the experience went. Darren realized something significant about his practice and was able to plan to adjust his approach to his teaching. This links in to the notion of developing professional values. Darren realized that the discussion of learning intentions and success criteria is much more important than he had appreciated prior to the peer learning interaction. It is interesting to see that he uses the word empowerment. This notion of reflection as something that can empower the person reflecting is a powerful argument for being part of the process. The sense of ownership too must make a big difference in terms of how the experience is interpreted by the person reflecting.

Finally, two quotes from BEd Primary Year 3 students:

I feel that this experience will better my teaching and development, I already feel more at ease about talking with a peer about my lesson, knowing that they will be honest and critical, and knowing that they can help me to improve my teaching just by thinking and talking about what I do, and why and how I do it.

This experience helped me to develop my reflective thinking. It enabled me to look objectively at my own teaching, and supported me when I applied the reflective questions to get my partner to reflect in the same way. (4th Year BEd Primary Students)

Summary

In this chapter, we looked at some responses to the peer learning inter-actions approach. Student teachers commented on the process and its benefits. They very much appreciated the opportunity to see another student in another context and to discuss their practice. The opportu-nity to talk to another student, who was at a similar point in their learn-ing, was another strength of this approach. In some cases students had adapted the approach to include an element of problem solving and advice in order to identify the next steps for professional learning.

All of the participants saw many advantages in the system, with many fully appreciating the opportunity to discuss their practice with-out having had the distracting, and often nerve-wracking, experience of having someone in to observe the actual lesson. We looked at a case study where a student teacher describes the benefits of discussing her practice when she had not been observed. There was also some discus-sion regarding the different approaches towards supporting student teachers out on placement. These were compared to the Peer Learning Interactions approach. Some student reflections were provided to sup-port the discussion.

Questions for Reflection

- List the advantages and disadvantages of this approach.
- Work with a partner and hold a peer learning interaction where you talk about something you have learned this week.
- Afterwards, discuss the process itself. Which questions worked best? How did you manage the 'silences'? Was it easy to listen and think of supplementary questions at the same time?
- Did you give advice or offer personal anecdotes instead of listen-ing and facilitating the learning for the other person?
- What would you do differently next time?

Further Reading

- Bolton, G. (2010) 'Reflection and reflexivity' (Chapter 2), *Reflective Practice*, 3rd edn. London: Sage.
- Brookfield, S. (1995) 'Learning to know ourselves' (Chapter 3), *Becoming a Critically Reflective Teacher*. San Francisco: Jossey-Bass.
- Moon, J. (1999) 'Learning through reflection', in Banks, F. and Shelton Mayes, A. (2001) *Early Professional Development for Teachers*. London: David Fulton/The Open University, Chapter 28.
- Mayes, A. (2001) *Early Professional Development for Teachers*. London: David Fulton/The Open University.

- Rollett, B. (1998) 'How do expert teachers see themselves?', in Banks, F. and Shelton Mayes, A. (2001) *Early Professional Development for Teachers*. London: David Fulton/The Open University, Chapter 4.

References

Boud, D. and Lee, A. (2005) 'Peer learning as pedagogic discourse for research education', *Studies in Higher Education*, 30(5): 501–16.

Ghaye, A. and Ghaye, K. (1998) *Teaching and Learning through Critical Reflective Practice*. Abingdon: David Fulton.

Ghaye, T. (2011) *Teaching and Learning through Critical Reflective Practice,* 2nd edn. David Fulton.

Kell, C., Fahnert, B., James, V. and Williamson, K. (2008) *Peer Review of Learning and Teaching: The Grass Roots Translating Policy into Innovative and Vibrant Practice*. Paper delivered to the HEA conference, Cardiff University, July.

Palmer, P. J. (1993) 'Good talk about good teaching: improving teaching through conversation and community', *Change*, 25: 8–13.

7

Reflective practice for children and young people

Chapter Overview

In this chapter, we will look at the idea of introducing a peer learning approach to reflection to primary school pupils, basically applying much of what we have been discussing in this book for professionals into a classroom context. If we can encourage pupils to stop, reflect on and talk about their learning, perhaps it will enable us to also develop the appropriate skills and attitudes. A pilot study was held in a local primary school, before the full study, looking at supporting pupils to develop their reflective skills. The study was based on the principle that if staff were engaged in 'teaching' pupils to engage in peer learning interactions, then they might themselves learn more about the process for themselves. Of course, the project also sought to benefit the pupils by helping them to develop vocabulary and skills for thinking and talking about their own practice, namely, their learning in school.

Such a project, if successful, might open the door to other contexts and other professions to use the peer learning interactions approach to encourage those participating to reflect, articulate and plan for professional development. This chapter covers:

- The pilot study
- Peer learning for pupils
- The full study
- Word list

This book is about developing reflective practice. So far we have looked at how important this can be and some of the ways that this is done. The focus of this book is the concept of reflection as an integral part of the teaching and learning process. It is well known that one of the best ways to learn and to understand what we know is to be in a position where we can teach others. Peer learning interactions seem one effective way to get professionals to engage with some meta-cognition in terms of their professionalism. Therefore, it makes sense to explore the possibility of putting these two ideas together. Perhaps we could use a peer learning approach to encourage meta-cognition for pupils. In order to do this, we would need to be thinking about the teaching and learning process as well as the experience of meta-cognition. Perhaps by going through the process of encouraging this with others, we might better understand it ourselves.

Although this book is aimed primarily at reflective practice and professionalism in teaching and working with children, it goes without saying that there is scope for using such an approach in other contexts and professions.

There have been many articles claiming that we remember best that which we learn by hearing, seeing and doing, and by teaching what we know. Therefore, we considered how we might develop an understanding of the process of reflection through introducing others to the process: 'children must think for themselves before they truly know and understand, and ... teaching must provide them with those linguistic opportunities and encounters which will enable them to do so' (Alexander, 2004: 12).

One way of teaching for meta-cognition is to make explicit and infuse the language of thinking and learning into the planning of teaching and into classroom discussion. The aim is to model the vocabulary we want children to use in their own thinking and understanding of learning by using it ourselves to describe our teaching, with such prompts as, 'The thinking we are going to be using today is ...', 'This lesson is about ...', 'What thinking have we been doing ...?' This will also involve the direct explanation of terms being used, and also challenging children to define these terms in their own words (Fisher, 1998). 'I think it is important because we think about what we are doing, and why we are doing it, and about how we are learning, and so we can help each other to learn better' (Primary school pupil, aged 10).

It may be that through teaching others to reflect on their learning, and through getting them to engage in the counselling model of supporting the articulation of those reflections, we might enhance our own skills and understanding and therefore become more able to engage in this kind of reflection ourselves.

If it were possible to encourage someone through this process of thinking about learning, and through articulating their thoughts about learning, and also give them support in developing the active listening skills and associated interview skills in the counselling mode described in this book, then perhaps we can achieve a much deeper understanding of the value and purpose of the reflective process. 'If we can bring the process of learning to a conscious level, we can help children to be more aware of their own thought processes and help them to gain control or mastery over the organisation of their learning' (Fisher, 1998).

In order to test this idea, my colleagues and I approached a local primary school with a proposal. We would spend some time teaching the pupils (aged 11) how to think and talk about their learning. Then we would teach them some of the skills of 'interviewing' so that they were able to 'get someone else talking'. The end product would be getting these pupils to visit younger children in the school (aged 7) and use these skills to encourage them to reflect on their own learning. My thinking was that in order to get the class to this stage the teacher and I would need to develop our own skills and understanding. Thus, the project would provide a context for the development of reflection and the awareness of meta-cognition for all concerned.

The Pilot Study

This early trial lasted about six weeks. We had three phases:

- thinking and talking about learning

- interview skills

- helping others to talk about their learning.

Thinking and talking about learning

We arrived in school at the end of a busy term with lots going on in school. We quickly realized that the pupils didn't really have the vocabulary to talk about their learning. If the project was going to be beneficial, then the class would need to be helped to identify the language of learning so that they had the tools to articulate their learning reflections. Although we put some effort into this task, we ran out of time on the pilot project and realized that this would take much longer to do effectively.

The problem of vocabulary is not confined to pupils in a primary school. If we want to encourage anyone to articulate their reflections, we do need to spend some time on establishing the kind of words, phrases, emotions, etc. that will be necessary to communicate these reflections. It may be that, in any context, time is devoted to establishing this vocabulary. The style and mode of reflection can be modelled; it can be described with examples. In the best scenarios, it would involve the participants establishing for themselves what the words and so on might be. Certainly, in the Initial Teacher Education context this would be a good starting point and perhaps, for some, the first step in terms of professional reflection.

> Although metacognitive knowledge may not depend on oral language ability, a robust vocabulary greatly helps young students develop and articulate it. As Bereiter and Scarmadalia (1983) observed, young children often lack the 'mentalistic vocabulary' needed to describe the events that occur in their own minds. Practice articulating these events, particularly when supported by an established collection of prompts or phrases, enables students to make their learning manifest to themselves and others. (Teachers College Record, 2009)

Indeed, within the pilot study we encouraged pupils to come up with a list of words and phrases to describe 'how they learn' and how they might feel about their learning. These were used as a starting point, a focus and later as a 'fallback' list to structure their reflections.

Interview skills

In terms of the interviewing, we also found that six weeks at the end of term were far from ideal. The pupils were very enthusiastic about the idea of interviewing their peers and especially excited about interviewing a younger pupil. We modelled some interviews and asked them to tell us what was good and what was not good in terms of interview skills. The class were then invited to come up with their own success criteria for a good interviewer.

They suggested that a good interviewer will:

- make eye contact

- look interested

- start with closed questions

- work up to open questions

- listen well and build connecting questions

- react positively

- smile and encourage.

They also acknowledged that some challenges for them might be:

- trying not to laugh

- thinking what to ask

- being able to think of 'piggy-back' questions

- holding and sorting out too many questions in your head

- feeling embarrassed and 'rubbish at this'.

The class then had the opportunity to practise these skills on each other to see how they fared. After a few opportunities doing this with their peers, it was time to work with a younger class.

Helping others to talk about their learning

Although they had thought about the relevant skills, and had had a couple of tries at doing this, interviews with the younger class did not work out as well as we had hoped. The pupils from both classes were very enthusiastic. Both sets of pupils gained a boost to their self-esteem and thoroughly enjoyed the interaction. However, the interviews turned out to be quite short and unfocused. The older pupils quickly ran out of questions to ask. The younger pupils felt awkward and were often reluctant to elaborate on their answers. The interactions degenerated into questions like: What is your favourite lesson? What else do you like doing? The younger pupils really struggled to talk about their learning.

Quotes from some of the older children who were engaged in this pilot activity:

It was impossible.

I kept asking the same question.

They kept saying yes or no.

I really enjoyed it.

It was kinda hard when you started off and then you started to get a bit more relaxed.

I find it quite awkward because Aaron kept looking down.

I thought I should ask him this question because he seemed to be in a world of his own.

I thought it better with these questions because making them up was hard.

This was, in part, down to the fact that they did not have the vocabulary to express themselves. They were unfamiliar with this kind of reflection and these kinds of interaction. It was also down to the fact that the interviewers themselves had had insufficient time to develop their skills and to know what to do when their younger partner 'froze' and had little to say.

Comments from their younger partners were:

It was awkward. There weren't many questions.

They asked weird questions/funny questions (unexpected).

It was nice. I don't see my buddy often.

The questions were familiar.

The pilot study established for us the need to ensure that pupils had sufficient understanding of the words to describe their own learning. It is not enough to assume that they will automatically be able to articulate what it is they feel they are learning, or, indeed, how they feel about the experience. This is something we decided to devote much more time and input into in the full study.

It is difficult to draw too many conclusions about the impact of our experiment on the teachers involved. One said that it had 'made me think a lot more about the learning words I use and ways I can help them to express themselves better'. Another reported that she had not only enjoyed working on 'teaching for good listening', but had also been forced to think about her use of questioning, and in particular her questioning in a facilitative manner, the suggestion here being that at least some of the associated skills were touched upon in this short experiment. The indications for reflection suggest that over a longer period perhaps the adults would develop peer learning skills at the same time as the pupils learn their meta-cognitive skills.

However, it is important to stress here that the difficulties the pupils might have had in finding the vocabulary for talking about their own learning might also apply to adults. Just as we might need to use, develop and 'teach' the appropriate vocabulary for them, so too we might need to support professionals in being able to articulate their reflections on their own practice.

Similarly, the interview skills were found lacking in our pilot. Again, we planned to improve upon this for our full study. Was this going to be an issue when doing this kind of thing with adults? Certainly in this book, I have tried to stress the importance of fully understanding the aims and processes associated with peer learning interactions. The skills of interviewing and the vocabulary of learning are crucial to the success of peer learning interactions, regardless of who the participants happen to be. It is also important for participants to be sure of their different roles and the kind of language required if they are to be free to articulate their reflections and their learning.

Peer Learning for Pupils

In Scotland, the Curriculum for Excellence (Scottish Government, 2007) is based around the philosophy that pupils have a sense of ownership of their learning and are involved in the decisions made about what they learn and how they learn it. The notion that learners have an investment in their own learning is one that is becoming more and more integrated into planning and teaching in Scotland.

One of the ways this is done is through sharing the dialogue of learning with a class at the start of a lesson, outlining what the learning will be and what 'success' will look like. In many schools now, pupils maintain a learning diary – sometimes called the learning log or Personal Learning Planning document (PLP for short). The idea here is for pupils to reflect upon their learning in any week and decide what their strengths and development needs might be.

> Personal learning planning represents an extension of self-assessment by students where they learn how to take greater responsibility for their learning in school and beyond.

> Three Rs – resilience, reflection and resourcefulness – provide an overarching framework within which to build an approach to personal learning planning using the principles and practice of formative assessment as presented in the Highland model. (Young, undated: 3)

For some years now, pupils have been writing down what they feel are their strengths and setting themselves targets for the week to come. The experience in our pilot study suggests that many children are still unsure about how to talk about their own learning. They are unsure too about 'how they learn' so planning next steps will be challenging for them.

> Students need to acquire a language for learning and for assessment to talk about what is to be learned and why, how it is being learned and how well.

> By approaching personal learning planning in this way, students can build gradually and securely the resilience, reflection and resourcefulness that will help them to pursue their own learning priorities at a later stage when they are ready to identify them by themselves. (Young, undated: 10)

It is hoped that the peer learning approach to reflection will help here. In the same way as the approach strives to encourage professionals to stop, reflect on and articulate what they learn about themselves and their own learning, so too could the approach be used for the benefit of pupils.

The Full Study

For our full study, we named the approach 'The Meta Learners Project'. With the tag 'meta learners are better learners', we went into school trying to promote the idea of reflection, peer learning, and the older pupils buddying the younger ones to support and encourage their thinking about their own learning.

In order to enable pupils to develop the vocabulary to talk about their own learning, it was important to have their teachers 'model' the language for them. One way of teaching for meta-cognition is to make explicit and infuse the language of thinking and learning into the planning of teaching and into classroom discussion. The aim is to model the vocabulary we want children to use in their own thinking and understanding of learning by using it ourselves to describe our teaching, with such prompts as 'The thinking we are going to be using today is …', 'This lesson is about …', 'What thinking have we been doing today…?' This will also involve the direct explanation of terms being used, and also challenging children to define these terms in their own words. Fisher (1998) expresses this very well and goes on to identify words that might scaffold pupils in their attempts to express their thinking about their learning.

Learning vocabulary

thinking learning understanding teaching mastering trying persevering wondering rehearsing practising modelling describing telling asking repeating exploring wondering investigating imagining creating listening choosing deciding planning assessing evaluating demonstrating explaining remembering talking discussing guessing predicting suggesting testing sketching checking considering reconsidering reviewing recalling noting noticing hypothesis idea summarizing etc. (Fisher, 1998)

Pramling, quoted in Fisher (1998), presents an analysis of an approach with children where 'there is a focus on thinking and where the significance of context is stressed. Children need this focus in order to articulate their thinking processes' (Pramling, 1998: 226–78).

Pramling suggests that there should be a focus on:

- *what* the child is thinking about a content – cognitive description (CD)

- *how* the child is thinking about the content – cognitive extension (CE)

- the child's thinking about his/her own thinking about the content – meta-cognitive thinking (MT).

If teachers can begin to use 'think-alouds' and to talk about thinking and ways of learning, then pupils will begin to learn the language of meta-cognition.

One way to raise awareness of such words in a classroom setting is to post a 'thinking word' relevant to a lesson on the board and to ask children to share definitions and applications of the word. Similarly, if we wish as a teacher or member of a teaching team to develop meta-cognition in our pupils, it might be helpful to create and share our own understanding or definition of 'meta-cognition' (Fisher, 1998).

Establish the language of learning

Teachers were given some key words about learning to discuss with the pupils. It was hoped that by exploring these 'learning words', they would be better prepared to understand them when they were modelled by the teacher and also that they might begin to use them when discussing their own learning. The word lists are listed below and also appear in the appendix, along with instructions for use in the classroom or with adult professionals as a focus for 'thinking and talking about our learning'.

Word List

Think and talk about the following:

Figure 7.1 Kinds of learning

wondering	exploring	thinking	trying out	testing
guessing	choosing	deciding	estimating	suggesting

Figure 7.2 Approaches to learning

trying	thinking	concentrating	using my plan
working out	problem-solving	trying different ways	remembering other learning
	taking care	making connections	

Figure 7.3 Group skills for learning

cooperating	being a good team member	sharing	considering others	supporting others

Figure 7.4 Review/reflection skills

remembering	checking		considering	noticing	improving
redrafting	showing others		adding more detail	making changes	making connections

Figure 7.5 How we feel about learning

confident	anxious	excited	bored	enthusiastic
happy	frustrated	confused	relaxed	curious

Some teachers posted all of the key words on their walls and periodically asked pupils to identify the most relevant for the learning that they were engaged in. Others decided to only present the word that was the focus at a particular time. Another teacher presented pupils with the word sheet (Appendix 5) and encouraged them to reflect at the end of each lesson and to highlight the kinds of learning they felt they had been doing.

One of the teachers had a list of 'how we learn' words on the wall with a personal copy for each child. For most lessons, she asked the pupils what and how they might be learning for that particular lesson: 'We look at the sheet and put a dot when we have been doing that kind of learning. We have lots of dots. There is almost a dot next to every word' (10-year-old pupil).

There are possibilities here for student teachers or other professionals to adapt the words to provide a reflective structure to use themselves in preparation for a professional reflection interaction. In Appendix 8, there is a suggested outline for introducing such an approach in a primary school class.

Developing the skills of listening and facilitating

When we introduced this project to the primary school pupils, we decided to separate the work on meta-language from the work on facilitating learning conversations. We felt that they needed to have a focus on each element first and then to put the two elements together only when they had had some experience of each.

Pupils were invited to watch some interviewing interactions and to comment on which skills were employed. Pupils quickly identified body language, facing the other person, looking interested, good eye contact, etc. They then witnessed two contrasting interviews where, in the first, the questions were mostly closed questions with a participant who wasn't interested in elaborating his answers. The second interview involved more open questions and a more willing partner. Pupils quickly identified the kinds of question that would get someone talking. Pupils were then given several opportunities to role play as interviewers and interviewees discussing such subjects as favourite holidays, best ever birthday, what I like on TV, to name but a few.

During a plenary session, the group decided that for an effective interview with someone you do not know well you should begin with some closed, factual questions before getting to the more open and cognitively challenging questions. The message that the point of the interview was to 'get the other person to talk' was clearly realized. The group also considered things they might do if the conversation got out of hand, off subject, or if it didn't get going in the first place.

Again, there is some relevance for peer learning interactions for adults.

It is important to put the other person at their ease, and to have something to ask if they do not feel able to 'get started' in their reflections.

Putting the two elements together

After some time spent practising using the language of learning and also developing interview skills, the time came to put these two elements together.

We returned to model some 'interviews about learning'. We chose one particular lesson to focus on and one person conducted a peer learning interaction with the pupils there as an audience. This was discussed in the light of what they had been doing on the project before we invited their own teacher to reflect on a lesson she had recently taught them. This was very useful as the pupils knew all about the lesson from their own perspective but enjoyed seeing their teacher reflect on and analyse what went well and what she would have liked to have done differently. Pupils then went into pairs to conduct a peer learning interaction discussing the same lesson.

More practice followed over the next few weeks. Finally, the pupils progressed to having these interactions with other pupils beyond their own classroom. They particularly enjoyed the challenge of conducting the sessions with classes of children who were much younger than themselves.

> It was good because you got to learn all about someone's hobby.
>
> It was OK, but I had to be with a girl!
>
> I liked talking about my reading with my buddy.

This was mutually beneficial as the younger pupils enjoyed the attention of a captive audience. Their self-esteem benefited in feeling that someone had the time and opportunity to listen to them talking about their learning without it being an adult who might have made them feel inhibited and intimidated. Those doing the facilitating also benefited as they developed their interview skills and were challenged to work to keep their partners talking. Sessions were only five minutes long but many of the younger pupils found this quite long enough.

One striking feature of the whole project was the way the pupils developed their own ability to think and talk about their own learning. Their interview skills also developed enormously and most were able to put aside their own egocentric approach to the world and to focus on 'getting others to speak'.

> My best question was, 'and is there anything else?'. Because when I run out of questions I ask it and then they suddenly have lots to add.
>
> Sometimes I think I should forget the questions and just say, 'is there anything about your learning that you would like to tell me!'

This project taught us a lot about learning and peer learning interactions. Teachers became more aware themselves of the language of learning and the many benefits of developing a meta-cognitive approach towards their teaching. In terms of the approaches advocated in this book, trialling the project with pupils revealed some important aspects of the skills and understanding essential for the approach in any context.

It is so important to have the language to discuss practice. It is important to have focus for the discussion and to sustain that focus. For the pupils, this meant having a range of starter questions and also some back-up questions for when things dried up or they went too far off the focus on learning. This is also true for adults, and the focus question sheet mentioned earlier in the book is one approach towards providing such a structure.

What the pupils said

When helping them it is important not to do it for them or tell them, instead you need to try to ask the questions so that they can find the answer themselves.

We did an interview about 'The Best Birthday Ever'. It was really good! We had to make up our own questions as we went along.

It was tricky trying to think of open questions so that they didn't just say 'yes' or 'no'.

We had a sheet on which to record the information that we gathered.

And then we had to write down our 'best' questions.

Sometimes it was hard to come up with questions to ask, we had to try to have open questions.

It would be good if we could make up questions first and then have them with us as a backup. If we got stuck then we could use them.

I liked the 'Birthday' one best because there was lots more to say about your best birthday and asking questions was much easier.

I liked making up my own questions, but did sometimes find it hard to ask open questions and not yes/no questions.

I liked asking questions and also being asked questions.

For the staff involved, the act of thinking the project through and implementing it brought reflection and the benefits of articulation to the fore and has provided them with a good deal of confidence and belief in the approach.

What the teachers said

As we progressed through the project I became much more aware of 'thinking about thinking' myself. In order to prepare the pupils for their metacognition I found myself reflecting on what it was I wanted them to do and

(Continued)

(Continued)

to learn. I was much more focused on the what, why and how of learning and teaching.

Later on when I was doing the peer learning interaction with my colleague, I found it much easier to put things into words. It was like I could see inside their heads and see the cogs working. I think also, the way the kids can now talk about what helps them to learn, and what gets in the way, makes it so much easier for me to do things that make a difference.

The whole idea of meta-cognition and reflective practice come together and support our development.

I was pleased with the class progress in such a short time. They could recall 'kinds of thinking' like: thinking, creating, working in groups and were quite comfortable in talking about them.

They also said that if someone looked at their class to see if they were learning, then the evidence of learning would be things like: pupils thinking, listening, working in groups, putting their hands up, etc. I thought that this demonstrated a good understanding of what the project was all about.

I was impressed that they had picked up the language and knew how to use it to articulate how they were learning.

They were aware of 'ways of learning' such as: how to know stuff, how to do stuff, what was wrong, what was right, creating, remembering, making, re-modelling.

They seemed quite savvy about the things that helped them to learn and the things that sometimes got in the way. It doesn't stop them being distracted but we now exchange lots of 'knowing looks'!

This approach towards introducing meta-cognition to children, and encouraging them to articulate their reflections on their learning, was a good way of introducing the concept and the approach to staff. Not only did the pupils benefit from the process and the skills that they learned, but also the staff involved were encouraged to think about reflection and articulation themselves. This in turn gave them the skills, the vocabulary and the hands-on experience to develop their own understanding and their abilities to develop reflective articulations for their professional development.

It was when Jamie was struggling to put into words the difficulties he was having in our gym lesson that I suddenly realised: this was exactly how I feel sometimes with my forward plans: trying to think about and improve too many things at once and succeeding with none of them. Imagine, being taught to professionally reflect by an eight-year-old!

Summary

In this chapter, we have looked at an approach where reflection about learning was introduced with primary school pupils. A similar approach was used to introduce it and there was a structured development of the relevant skills. Teachers learned a lot from taking their classes through the process and their own meta-cognition about reflection was increased. Although this chapter is about 'doing it for the kids', it does demonstrate that one way of improving your own reflection is to encourage others to reflect on their learning. We identified the challenges for such an approach and the problems of 'thinking of questions to ask', and 'I couldn't get her to talk about her learning for long' will apply, not just to children, but also to seasoned professionals.

Questions for Reflection

- Consider what you might learn from what pupils said about their reflective experiences. Think about what was said about the 'language of learning', and the vocabulary for expressing our reflections.
- Consider how you might develop your own skills via the experience of teaching it to others. Is there an opportunity in your context for this to happen? If you are a teacher or student, can you implement such a project in your school?
- Consider the resources used in this project – can they be adapted/improved on for your own use?

Further Reading

- Alexander, R. (2004) *Towards Dialogic Teaching: Rethinking Classroom Talk.* Dialogos, pp. 9–16.
- Brookfield, S.D. (1995) 'Holding critical conversations about teaching', Chapter 7 in *Becoming a Critically Reflective Teacher.* San Francisco: Jossey-Bass.

- Devereux J. (2001) 'Pupils' voices: discerning views on teacher effectiveness', Chapter 20 in F. Banks and A. Shelton Mayes (eds) *Early Professional Development for Teachers*. London: David Fulton/The Open University.
- Fisher, R. (1998) 'Thinking about thinking: developing metacognition in children', *Early Child Development and Care*, 141: 1–15. Available at: www.teaching-thinking.net/thinking/web%20resources/robert_fisher_thinkingaboutthinking.htm
- Swartz, R.J. and Parks, S. (1994) *Infusing the Teaching of Critical and Creative Thinking into Content Instruction*. Pacific Grove, CA: Critical Thinking Books & Software.
- Swartz, R.J. and Perkins, D.N. (1989) *Teaching Thinking: Issues and Approaches*. Cheltenham, Australia: Hawker Brownlow Education.

References

Alexander, R. (2004) *Towards Dialogic Teaching: Rethinking Classroom Talk*. Dialogos.

Fisher, R. (1998) 'Thinking about thinking: developing metacognition in children', *Early Child Development and Care*, 141: 1–15. Available at: www.teachingthinking.net/thinking/web%20resources/robert_fisher_thinkingaboutthinking.htm

Pramling, I. (1998) 'Developing children's thinking about their own learning'. *British Journal of Educational Psychology*, 58: 226–78.

Scottish Government (2007) *A Curriculum for Excellence*. Available at: www.scotland.gov.uk/Resource/Doc/26800/0023690.pdf

Teachers College Record (2009) Volume 111, Number 8, pp. 1997–2020. Available at: www.tcrecord.org (accessed 24 May 2011).

Young, E. (undated) *Learning and Teaching Reflection Framework: Learning Dispositions and Personal Learning Planning*. Highland Council Education Department. http://www.highland.gov.uk/NR/rdonlyres/6A43ABC4-6125-4716-ABB2-85735F9F8760/0/LearningDispositionsandplpingSept092.pdf

How do we support putting reflection into practice?

Chapter Overview

In this chapter, we will investigate how we might begin to turn 'talking about practice' into taking action to improve practice. It is all very well to stop and reflect on practice, but it is quite another thing to move from reflection to action. This chapter will cover:

- From reflection into practice
- Reflection: total success?
- Reflection: partial success?
- Reflection: mostly challenging?
- Looking for support
- Reflection: experimenting?
- Practice making sense of practice
- What might it look like?
- Changing practice, changing attitudes, changing values

From Reflection into Practice

Turning talking about practice into actions that will improve practice is the focus of this chapter. As McGhie and Barr have said:

> Making this happen requires opportunities for significant discussions and debate, and schools to learn to ask themselves the kind of questions to which they best know the answers. They need to learn how to step back and ask reflective

questions. 'Where are we at compared with where we want to be?' 'What are the possibilities for next steps?' 'What unexpected directions can we see that hadn't occurred to us before?' 'Why did that avenue of approach not work?' 'What kind of help do we need now to make progress?' 'What resources do we need?' (McGhie and Barr, 2001: 79)

Making this happen in practice is the challenge and the opportunity for all teachers. In its report of 2011, the Scottish Government suggested that:

> Tailoring CPD closely to the needs of individual schools and teachers and using coaching and practical activities using real examples rather than 'input' (*from external agencies*) is effective in increasing the confidence of teachers to implement the new curriculum. This combination of tailored CPD which meets individual needs in-house, is peer-led and sustained through professional dialogue, with some specialist input to provide an external perspective where appropriate, seems an effective and efficient way to continue to support teachers. (Scottish Government, 2011: 69)

The terms 'peer-led' and 'tailored to individual needs' fit well with the models of reflection discussed in this book and would equip more teachers and professionals to take part in professional articulations leading to reflection and development of practice. The report goes on to state that: 'mentoring and coaching skills enable much more effective dialogue and learning to take place within groups of teachers and with stakeholders and partners'. And unequivocally the suggestion is that: 'all teachers should see themselves as teacher educators and be trained in mentoring' (Scottish Government, 2011: 73).

Therefore, there is a very definite steer, in Scotland at any rate, to become involved in reflection and in supporting our fellow professionals in those reflections. The 'thinking through and articulating' approach to reflective practice is one way of beginning to address this mentoring training advocated by the Scottish government.

The view here, on reflection being part of professionalism, with a focus on the practitioner already established in their workplace, still has a bearing if you are still at the early stages of your professional career. After all, if you can consider the concept of reflection as an integral part of professional practice right from the beginning of your career, then you will not have the same problems that are experienced by seasoned professionals who have rarely been asked to articulate these professional reflections during the whole of their career so far. The significance of the ideas espoused in this book for emerging professionals and students is that it is important to start out with the right frame of mind when it comes to reflection. Yet, it is because we know that there are many professionals out there, who rarely reflect with any structure or intent, that this book strives to target both audiences.

Reflection: Total Success?

The result of thinking through your practice might simply be, to keep on doing what you were doing before. After all, some of the time we get it right, don't we?

Yet there is still something different about 'doing the same' when you have reflected on what it is that you did and why you think it worked so well. This meta-cognition means that the probability of repeating your success is much higher. Knowing why it worked so well means that you can focus on replicating the factors in order to repeat success. It also means that you can devote your attention to other elements of practice which may not have gone so well.

> Reflective practice involves 'noticing aspects of (their) own practice' perhaps triggered by some form of surprise, or by some question from an external observer, they recognize and work on issues and concerns. Their thinking, reinforced, possibly by its articulation, puts them in a more knowledgeable position for future decision making and professional action. (Jaworsky, 1993: 37–42)

It may be that the success. on this one occasion, may have lessons that are transferable to other times, other places, other contexts. Such learning can then be applied elsewhere. For example, in teaching you might try a new way of organizing resources and their distribution. If it works well, then acknowledging this and reflecting on how success came about might inform your practice so that in other lessons, with other materials, a similar approach could be employed.

 Example: case study

Caroline, a primary school teacher of 6-year-olds, discusses the benefits of analysing the success of her approach:

> We did a modelling activity where we demonstrated how to sort the information and put it into a Venn diagram. It was interesting to look back and see how we had to almost spell it out to the kids so that they could understand the process. Looking back it worked really well – there was a real logic about it that we were able to demonstrate. The proof of its success came the day after when the groups had to try to do the same thing independently. It worked really well. They were able to follow all of the steps in the way we had shown them. The satisfying thing for me was that because we had talked about it I had a better understanding as to why it worked so well!

Reflection: Partial Success?

On the other hand, reflection might enable us to focus on an element of practice which requires some attention. It might be that practice was mostly good, but there is just the one niggling thing that needs attention. In such circumstances, it is important initially to identify what went well and why. Often this can provide the key to unlocking a way forward with the 'niggle'. 'Talking to colleagues helps us to become aware of how much we take for granted in our own teaching ... it confirms the correctness of instincts that we felt privately but doubted because we thought they contradicted conventional wisdom' (Brookfield, 1995: 141).

It is also important not to throw the baby out with the bathwater. It is important not to allow the niggle to distract us from the 'good practice'. Reflecting on the good and the routine is just as important as reflecting on the frustrations of practice. There are many elements of practice that work and which we take for granted, yet with some reflection we can move beyond 'blind acceptance' and into a deeper critical understanding. Bolton (2010: 48) explains: 'Reflection and reflexivity critique anything taken for granted. We need to walk away from things, to gain perspective. Why? How? What? Who? Where? and When? need to be asked of everything, constantly.'

Ghaye and Ghaye echo this belief:

> Reflective practice is a process which involves a reflective turn. This means returning to look again at all our taken-for-granted values, professional understandings and practices. This focus on routines, rituals, on everyday occurrences that make up the bulk of the working day is most important. Reflecting on practice is not about reflecting only on the extraordinary, the exceptional and the 'one-off'. (1998: 16)

 Example: case study

Carol Ann, a primary school teacher of 8-year-olds, discusses the benefits of analysing the success of her approach:

> We went over the art activity. I showed everyone the technique. Through questioning I felt sure that everyone knew what they were supposed to be doing. Yet when they went back to their seats Michael and John just didn't seem to know what they were doing. They stuck

everything down in the wrong place and looked genuinely surprised when I exploded at them for not listening.

When I reflected on this with my learning partner I realized that it wasn't the activity that was wrong, or even my approach, but something else. It may be that I was happy to be fooled into thinking that they all understood, just because collectively they answered my questions, or it could be that those particular pupils find holding instructional information too challenging.

Anyway, through discussion and planning how to move forward with my reflections I decided that I needed to provide some of the pupils with a more practical way of remembering what to do.

The next week when we did the next lesson in the art sequence I got Michael and John to do the demonstration while I provided a commentary. Through actually experiencing the instructions, with scaffolded support, they were able to remember afterwards just how to go about things.

I think that the reflection session enabled me to step back from my own frustrations about their seeming inability to listen, and to come up with something that not only supported them (Michael and John) but also the other pupils in that lesson, and also ... it gave me a strategy to use in other situations with other pupils who find instructional support challenging.

Reflection: Mostly Challenging?

Sometimes things really do not go to plan. In any profession, there can be times when the frustration of things not going to plan can be such that there is a smokescreen which prevents us from seeing clearly any other options or ways of doing things. In such circumstances, a professional reflection interaction might provide the platform for evaluating and analysing what is actually going on that is inhibiting progress or success. It is important to try to establish/identify the problem.

Typical questions might be:

- What element of practice is it that is not working?
- Has this happened before? If so, are there parallels to it?
- How did you advance things the last time?
- If this is unique, is it to do with the individuals concerned? Is it likely to be repeated?

(Continued)

> *(Continued)*
>
> - If there is a recurring problem, how can you unpack what is happening and why it is happening?

The next step is to consider how to solve the problem. Can you reflect on what happened, how you might try to do things differently?

> - Describe what you did, what they did and where the frustration lies.
> - Is there a trigger for when things start to slide?
> - What can you change about the organization that might help?
> - Is there anything about the timing, pace and approach you might change?
> - What about yourself – can you adopt a different attitude or adapt your persona so that you come across in a different way?

It may be that you have tried everything you can come up with. It is important at this stage to consider whether the changes needed are within your control. Think about the factors which you can change, and those you cannot. If there are factors that you feel you cannot change, then a whole new approach may be needed. In most cases, professionals do come up with solutions or at least ideas that they can try, but when these prove to be elusive the next step is to seek a solution elsewhere.

Looking for Support

The next steps then are to consider where you might find a solution. There are many resources available, whatever profession you are in, here are some:

> - other professionals in the same situation
> - more experienced professionals whom you might ask
> - other adults, who, although not in the same profession, might bring a fresh insight into the problem
> - books and sources of information such as the internet
> - research documents and journals
> - 'how to' videos and DVD clips.

One benefit of having had a peer learning interaction is that you will be much more focused in your quest for support. You will be able to articulate exactly what the problem is and know the kind of support that you need. It should be possible, through articulating your reflections, to explain what kind of support you are looking for and how it might apply to your particular situation.

Example: case study

Simon, reflecting on a lesson on imaginative writing with a primary school teacher of 10-year-olds:

> Simon was articulating his reflections on his lesson on popular culture. He reflected that he had, in looking back, not been quite clear about his learning intentions and success criteria. He had his idea of what the pupils would get out of his lesson but they had a different interpretation.
>
> Through reflecting he realized that he needed a new approach to ensure that in future there was a clear understanding of what the class were to do and what they were to learn.
>
> Although he and his learning partner discussed this at length, the plan that emerged from the interaction was that he, himself would go back to basics.
>
> He went to the library and found a number of books and journals on formative assessment. Having clarified his understanding he came back to discuss with his learning partner what he had learned and how he planned to use this knowledge to influence his own practice.
>
> The result was a different approach at the start of his lessons where the learning was made more explicit and the pupils were involved in identifying what 'success' might look like.
>
> The reflection, the discussion and the reference to literature and research are all elements of his developing professionalism. It must be acknowledged that for Simon the approach he adopted post-reflection was not something totally new. He had been taught the theory some time ago. He had read the books and even started his teaching with emphasis on the learning intentions and success criteria. However, it was something he had done, not fully understanding why and how it was important. Through his experience in the focus lesson and the subsequent peer learning interaction he realized what he did not know and understand. Thereafter he was able to return to the information and absorb it in the light of his teaching experience. Hence he now has a much firmer grasp of what it all means.
>
> The impact of this reflection had an effect beyond the single lesson that was the focus of his peer learning interaction.

This is an excellent example of the way reflection can link into professional development and can inform improvements in practice – not just for one particular lesson, but for a whole pedagogical approach. This is supported by Forde and O'Brien (2011: 30) where they suggest that 'the crucial aspect is not just a process of reflection on experience but the seeking and using of a range of sources of knowledge including theoretical and research-based knowledge in order to ground learning and practice in a sound theoretical frame'.

As suggested elsewhere, this process of reflection and the seeking of sources of knowledge does not need to be something done alone in isolation. Through work with a peer, there can be a joint exploration of knowledge and this in turn may lead to joint planning for development in practice as described earlier in terms of learning rounds and for lesson study.

Pendlebury (1995) describes the peer supporter or facilitator as the 'dialogical other':

> Reflective practice is much more than a method. It is a self reflective practice that chooses something significant to know about or do something with, and which is directed and energized by interest and insight. It is the way individuals, groups or organizations reflect on information generated through the use of particular methods. It is influenced by our capacity to openly dialogue with the information we have gathered through the use of particular methods (and) it is the way we use the above to enable us to question what it is we claim we are coming to know. (Ghaye, 2011: 35)

Brookfield (1995: 42) considers this reflection as a fundamental element of development:

> In the aftermath of action, we try to find the opportunity to reflect back on the memories, experiences, and interpretations that caused us to make what felt like instinctive responses ... good teaching becomes synonymous with a continuous and critical study of our reasoning processes and our pedagogic actions.

He goes on to suggest that:

> Critical reflection is a matter of stance and dance. Our stance towards our practice is one of enquiry. We see it as being in constant formation and always needing further investigation. Our dance is the dance of experimentation and risk. (Brookfield, 1995: 42)

Reflection: Experimenting?

Sometimes professional development can be elusive, however. Not all problems come with a handy solution. It is often the case that reflection brings with it the identification of problems or situations to which there are no simple answers. It may be that the standard approaches and resources just don't fit the situation you find yourself in. It may be that the individuals involved, or even the limitations of your own personal repertoire of strategies, present a barrier to success.

It is these very situations that give creativity an enormous opportunity. Creative responses are sometimes required to explore 'other ways of working'. However, along with this comes the need to experiment and to try things that have no guarantee of success. In modern professional practice, there needs to always be room for some experimentation. The kind of reflection process advocated in this book should provide a secure base from which to work.

If the reflection has taken place with a peer, and a plan has been arrived at to improve a situation, it should also be the case that this experiment can be implemented without fear of failure or censure. Certainly, for students and emerging professionals this creative experimental phase is essential if they are going to develop their own identity and sense of practice as a collaborative, imprecise art, where there are few definitive sure-fire answers to every problem.

Providing that the experiment has been thought through and is in response to the reflections on practice, this approach has much to offer. The fact that it is the result of genuine self-initiated professional reflection and that it has been planned and thought through, then the person involved should have less sense of a fear of failure and more of a notion of pioneering a solution for a given problem. Having worked through this experiment with a peer means that there is support and further opportunities to explore this element of their practice safe from judgement and fear of failure.

Ghaye and Ghaye (1998: 22) discuss this risk taking as a creative enterprise:

> Making sense needs to be viewed as an active and creative process of jointly constructed interpretations (Newman and Holzman, 1997).

> Knowledge generated through reflective conversations is a creative and constructivist process and one 'that construes learning as an interpretive, recursive, building process by active learners interacting with the physical and social world' (Fosnot, 1996: 30).

Example: case study

Mike discussed the problems he was having with his class of 7-year-olds. They were very noisy and boisterous when they lined up to come into school every morning.

> It feels like each day begins with a battle and then things just go downhill from there.

In his peer learning session he discussed this and various ideas for improving the situation. He went away to do some research, asking around for suggestions he came up with a suggestion which, for him, was quite radical. Mike decided to experiment with a start to his day where the class did not line up at all. Instead he allowed them to come into school at any time from 8.50 to 9.00. He provided calming music and paper and colouring pens at their desks.

> I was very nervous about how it would go and how they would react, but I needn't have worried. The kids loved it! They were so calm! There was no pushing to be first in the lines. They had the chance to come in and chat quietly – catching up with their friends. Most of them didn't even need the colouring option. It was a radical risk but it paid off. We are all so much more relaxed in the morning. It's a much better starting point for the day!

Mike went through the process of professional reflection. He tried to resolve his frustrations and ended up going elsewhere for ideas. He then came back with his 'radical' plan. His peer learning partner gave him the confidence to experiment and try something different, free from the fear of judgement or failure. In the end, his idea worked and he could move on. This is professional reflection in practice – making a difference for all concerned. 'Reflective conversations can also be viewed as empowering ... in helping them [the teachers] control their own behaviours and becoming more aware of what they are doing' (Ghaye and Ghaye, 1998: p23).

Practice Making Sense of Practice

Many professionals lament the lack of time for reading about the latest thinking and new ideas about their practice. For many, the longer they are in the job the less they have the opportunity to stop and look at how the theory is changing. Although many professions do have mechanisms for promoting the latest thinking, from in-service sessions to management dictates, encouraging staff to become familiar with certain initiatives, most would say that they simply do not have the time. Another problem is that most of us get so involved in the day-to-day pressures of the job that we do not have the 'space' to consider what is going on in the development of our profession.

Perhaps peer learning interactions can help here. Sessions might focus on reading and discussion about how ideas read about might influence practice. Perhaps the identification of development needs can promote an interest in reading up on the latest ideas on how to approach things differently, just like in some of the case studies mentioned in this chapter.

It may be that having discussed something with a fellow professional one might be more inclined to make time to read the theories that help us to make sense of our reflections.

> Change, it has been said, is the only constant, in education and in society generally. When those affected by changes feel an inability to influence the impact on their lives, change becomes disempowering. If we can give the stakeholders in schools a full part in the process, it is more likely that it will forge stronger relationships among the various groups and lead to action which is lasting and sustainable. (MacBeath et al., 1996: 75)

Setting targets

As discussed elsewhere in this book, it is important to work towards turning reflection into practice. The cycle of reflection, discussion and then target setting has been explored. It might be that reference to different theories or resources can enable a more informed look forwards, building on reflection into developing practice.

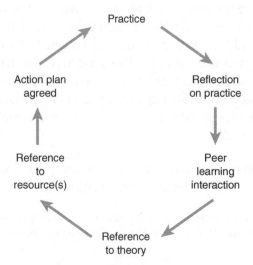

Figure 8.1 Reflective cycle

Using resources

This cycle of approach is beneficial in terms of using new resources to support identified needs in the classroom. It might be useful in a similar way in other professions. Once a need has been identified, then reading can be done to find out possible solutions and approaches. Inevitably, this might involve investigating resources and new methodology in order to experiment and see if such support will help to develop practice.

This could also be useful as a means of exploring the potential of new resources and different approaches. Even if it is not introduced as a response to professional reflections and a perceived need, new resources might be introduced at the start of the cycle (shown above) and the reflections can be focused upon how well they supported practice.

Advice, support, teamwork

It may be that the peer learning interaction identifies the need for advice or support from a more experienced professional. They then would become the 'resource' indicated in the cycle.

The advice given and the action plan jointly constructed would then go on to support experiments to develop practice. The cycle would continue with the practice reflected upon, and conclusions could be made about the advice given and evaluations could be made about the impact on practice.

It may be that teamwork or collaborative work is the method used for identifying next steps. Or the 'lesson study', which we explored in Chapter 2, could be selected as the way forward. If so, then the cycle would be adapted accordingly. The reflective practitioner is in this sense represented as 'an intellectually curious person who rejects a passive approach to knowledge and prefers to construct knowledge together with others rather than simply "consume" it' (Reed and Canning, 2010: 15).

Ghaye and Ghaye present a version of the peer learning approach where they describe 'reflective conversations':

> Reflective conversations may initially take the form of 'private conversations with self', but then they should be articulated in public company. In doing

this, teachers can describe, explain and justify practice and when appropriate persuade, confront and encourage others to question their own practice. This ... (can provide an) opportunity to reflect upon and to shape their own work and, in certain circumstances, transform what they do, so as to improve educational experiences of the children in their care. (Ghaye and Ghaye, 1998: 20)

These 'reflective conversations,' and 'private conversations' are not unlike the idea of the 'peer learning interactions' and 'professional monologues' used to explore reflection described in this book.

What Might it Look Like?

When we looked at possible pro formas for recording peer learning interactions in Chapter 5, we touched upon the idea that we might need to make a plan of action to follow on from what we learned. It may be that in such an action plan the need to research other ideas and approaches will be recorded. This provides evidence of professional development and will be a reminder for subsequent interactions. It might be that later on the topic will be returned to with a particular focus on the research/reading and an evaluation of how this might inform future practice. It might link into a 'lesson study' approach or a 'learning rounds' approach, in order to experiment with new approaches to practice in a supportive way. However, this will be a very 'real' and authentic way to engage with these approaches, as it will be in response to an identified need that arises out of personal professional reflections.

Changing Practice, Changing Attitudes, Changing Values

Change needs commitment. Teachers and schools will not change unless they share a compelling reason for doing so. They need to have some say in how that change will be brought about. They need to be able to picture for themselves how that change will affect them personally. They need to understand that change does not mean more work, just different work. (McGhie and Barr, 2001: 79)

If we are going to influence any kind of personal or institutional change, it is essential that we feel some sense of ownership of the process and direction of change. Rather than receiving dictates from elsewhere, it is important for professionals to have some sense of control. Perhaps through reflective practice, however structured or arrived at, we can be fully aware of our strengths and development needs; we might be more able to think and talk about our profession in a way which articulates what it is that needs to 'stay the same' and what it is that needs to change. Furthermore, perhaps such reflection will give a structure to a *process* for making that change happen – based on a shared understanding, the latest research and critical thinking, and supported by a collegiate approach to experimenting and developing professional practice.

Of course, there will always be barriers to change and those resistant to trying anything new or unconventional. Changing attitudes and values is not something done overnight. Indeed it is not something to be done lightly. However, for most of us it is enough to take those first steps to stop, reflect on what we do, consider why and how we do it, and then make informed decisions about our best way forward. The approaches discussed in this book rely on a high level of self-motivation and no little support from at least one fellow professional. Success would depend on that commitment to reflect and develop, and support will depend upon having that colleague who has the same dedication and trust. 'Self-evaluation will work only where there is a climate of trust and where the agenda is openly agreed. This involves the willing participation of the various groups, with a clear and unambiguous agreement about purpose and outcomes' (MacBeath et al., 1996: 76).

Summary

In this chapter, we considered how we might move from reflection into practice. We looked at some case studies from teachers who were experiencing challenges in their day-to-day practice and how they found support in articulating their situation, taking advice from others, and through researching new approaches. We looked at the different sources of support available and ways of taking this support and turning it into some kind of action plan for implementation.

The chapter stressed that changing values and attitudes is a long and difficult process, and that change comes about when individuals feel some ownership for it, and understand why and how change might happen. Above all, change needs to be seen as beneficial and supportive rather than externally imposed and unexplained. The reflective process, combined with reference to fellow professionals and current literature on practice, is one which might provide authentic professional development for individuals and institutions which is effective, meaningful and relevant.

〰️ Questions for Reflection

- Consider the case studies discussed in this chapter. To what extent do you see them as typical examples of reflection in practice? Try to think of situations where you had a similar experience in reflecting on what and how you were doing and deciding to consider other ways and approaches.
- Consider something that you did well and on reflection made a conscious decision to repeat on another occasion, thus enabling reflection to inform future practice.
- Think about your emerging professional values. Do you do things on the basis of thought and professional discussion, or do you do them because that's the way you were shown how?
- Take one element of your practice and try to stop, think, reflect, articulate – what, why, how you do what you do?
- Think about the support and resources available to you in your profession. Ask yourself if you have drawn on this support recently. Do you make enough use of this support and these resources? If not, why not? Might such reflections be more productive in a peer learning interaction with a colleague?

Further Reading 📖

- Blandford, S. (2001) 'Professional development in schools', Chapter 2 in F. Banks and A. Shelton Mayes (eds) *Early Professional Development for Teachers*. London: David Fulton/The Open University.
- Brookfield, S.D. (1995) 'What it means to be critically reflective', Chapter 1 in *Becoming a Critically Reflective Teacher*. San Francisco: Jossey-Bass.
- Mercer, N. and Dawes, L. (2001) 'Dialogues for teaching and learning', Chapter 14 in F. Banks and A. Shelton Mayes (eds) *Early Professional Development for Teachers*. London: David Fulton/The Open University.
- Munro, J. (2001) 'Learning more about learning improves teacher effectiveness', Chapter 18 in F. Banks and A. Shelton Mayes (eds) *Early Professional Development for Teachers*. London: David Fulton/The Open University.

References

Bolton, G. (2010) *Reflective Practice: Writing and Professional Development*, 3rd edn. London: Sage.

Brookfield, S. D. (1995) *Becoming a Critically Reflective Teacher*. San Francisco: Jossey-Bass.

Forde, C. and O'Brien, J. (2011) 'Policy and practice in education', no.29. *Coaching and Mentoring: Developing Teachers and Leaders*. Edinburgh: Dunedin Academic Press.

Fosnot, C. (ed) (1996) *Constructivism: Theory, Perspectives and Practice.* New York: Teachers College Press.

Ghaye, A. and Ghaye, K. (1998) *Teaching and Learning through Critical Reflective Practice.* London: David Fulton.

Jaworsky, B. (1993) 'Professional development of teachers: the potential of critical reflection', *British Journal of Inservice Education,* 19: 37– 42.

MacBeath, J., Boyd, B., Rand, J. and Bell, S. (1996) *Schools Speak for Themselves.* London: The National Union of Teachers.

McGhie, M. and Barr, I. (2001) 'Learning and ethos', in *Turning the Perspective.* Enschede, The Netherlands: Consortium of Institutions for Development and Research in Education in Europe/Netherlands Institute for Curriculum Development (CIDREE/SLO).

Newman, F. and Holzman, L. (1997) *The End of Knowing: A New Developmental Way of Knowing.* London: Routledge.

Pendlebury, S. (1995) 'Reason and story in wise practice', in H. McEwan and K. Egan (eds) *Narrative in Teaching, Learning and Research.* New York: Teachers College Press.

Reed, M. and Canning, N. (2010) *Reflective Practice in the Early Years.* London: Sage.

Scottish Government (2011) *Teacher Education in Scotland: The Report Setting out the Findings of the Review of Teacher Education.* Edinburgh: Scottish Government.

Reflecting on reflections: reflections on reflecting

> ## Chapter Overview
>
> This chapter considers:
>
> - Through the mirror
> - The challenges and frustrations of reflective practice
> - Who is it all for?
> - A management role?
> - Variations
> - Reflecting on reflections
> - Combining roles

Looking into a mirror, we see a reflection of what is. Reflective practice might begin here, but it needs to go much further. These reflections of 'what is' need to be held up to scrutiny. They might need some 'air-brushing' to modify blemishes. They might need some things to be changed in order to present a more representative view. They may need certain aspects to be accentuated in order to do justice to the image presented. The view might identify some development needs in order to represent the image before you. Whilst not looking to be 'the fairest of them all', we all strive, professionally, to be all that we can be.

Through the Mirror

In this book, we have explored a number of approaches to reflection and to professional development. Of course, using the word 'reflection' wasn't the right way to describe peer learning interactions. A reflection merely reflects what is, it doesn't go beyond the present and point the way to the future. In Gillie Bolton's book on reflective practice, she talks about 'through the mirror' writing. Her idea is that we need to look through the mirror, not at it. Looking at it merely reflects what is there:

> Other methods of reflection help practitioners to look in the mirror and see an image of themselves reversed, but otherwise just the same. Through the mirror writing … is so called because writers are taken right through the mirror's glass and silvering to a reflective and reflexive world where nothing can be taken for granted. (Bolton, 2010: xxi)

As we have looked at the different ways of reflecting, it has become clear that reflection is no simple thing. It means different things to different people depending on what they are looking for and why they are looking. For some, it is about finding a way to stop and think about their practice; at what works well and what might be improved. For others, it might be more to do with looking for professional support, where someone is willing to listen, to understand and not to judge. Then there are those who see it as yet another imposition from management, trying to make them more accountable. Or they see it as a chore, imposed upon staff who feel overworked, undervalued and far too busy to stop and take part.

Having looked at the theory and the evidence presented in this book, it would be difficult to argue against the benefits claimed on behalf of professional reflection, yet reflection is the term used commonly in most professions. A more accurate picture of reflection is provided by Ghaye and Ghaye:

> Reflective practice needs to be understood as a discourse (Fairclough, 1998). A discourse can be understood as a set of meanings, statements, stories and so on to produce a series of events. The reflective discourse, or conversation has the potential to disturb our professional identity and those things that give our teaching its shape, form and purpose. (1998: 16)

> This posture is not one that should be exclusively backward looking with the conversation being preoccupied with explorations and justifications of previous practice. Reflective conversations should also be forward looking and be conversations of both possibility and hope. (1998: 21)

How you teach is very much bound up in 'who you are'; it is about personal and professional identity. Through seeing others teach, listening and talking to others about teaching, values and attitudes are formed and developed. If this process can be encouraged in a climate of trust and away from the inhibitions of judgement and accountability, perhaps progress will be swift and more enduring. For those setting out on their professional development, this is a crucial phase. For other, more experienced professionals, it might be the opportunity you need to check out your values and taken-for-granted ways of doing things. Either way, reflective practice, and in particular the articulation of these reflections, is a powerful thing.

In this book, we have considered the relationship between reflective practice and professionalism. We have looked at the many different approaches, their strengths and weaknesses, and also considered some real-life responses to the act of reflection. As well as looking at these benefits, however, the book has also attempted to take on board the criticisms and challenges of reflecting on practice. In particular, this book has looked at what practitioners see as the drawbacks and frustrations of reflective practice.

The Challenges and Frustrations of Reflective Practice

There are a number of frustrations that get in the way of regular, meaningful reflection. Despite a professional understanding and a need to take part, there are still a number of challenges which get in the way:

It doesn't help me in my day-to-day practice.

I don't have the time.

What's the point in doing it once a year and then doing nothing about it?

I wouldn't know how to begin.

What's the point in identifying my needs if nobody can help me to work on them when I find them?

Why would I want to stop and tell management about my weaknesses if they then use them against me?

Why do we need yet more management-led bureaucratic impositions just so somebody somewhere can tick a box to say, we've done it?

Such criticisms have been explored and possible solutions offered. Certainly the focus for this book has been to evaluate how we can have a form of reflection which feels less threatening and imposed, and more personal and supportive. Peer learning interactions seek to offer a less time-consuming approach where the subject doesn't feel judged.

This approach has been presented with feedback from students, teachers and pupils and all seemed to value the experience as an opportunity for free autonomous reflection.

In writing this book I, myself, have been forced to reflect upon reflection itself. Through researching current practice and consulting with students and teachers about the methods and implications of professional reflection, I have come to better understand many of its benefits and challenges. As a colleague in a local primary school expressed it: 'It is quite a shift in thinking for some staff to realise that through reflection they can take control of what they are doing in the classroom and become more confident in reflecting and discussing this with others' (Dianne, primary school teacher).

It seems so easy to demonstrate the *value* of reflecting and then move on to develop practice. It is easy to convince others that it is worthwhile and that it will not take up too much of their valuable time. What is difficult, however, is trying to change the culture so that such reflection becomes part of practice, and not simply an add-on, an afterthought, an extra that we know we ought to do but which we rarely get around to. There is something of an ironic contradiction here, if we have to *enforce* reflective interactions. One premise of this book is that the best, most effective reflections come when participants set their own agenda, free from ideas and ideology imposed on them from management. It suggests that students and teachers work best in the absence of authority figures and that they are more likely to experiment and develop practice if they feel free from the fear of failure. 'In other words someone telling us about the positive outcomes regarding reflection as peers wasn't enough, we had to do it for ourselves, become part of it and take ownership for it to have meaning and relevance' (Dianne, primary school teacher).

And yet it has to be said that there is a huge culture change needed if we are to develop reflective practice which goes beyond the 'bolt-on' approach. 'Reflective practice and reflexivity are states of mind, an ongoing constituent of practice, not a technique, or curriculum element, but a pedagogical approach which should "pervade the curriculum"' (Fanghanel, 2004: 576).

However, we should, perhaps, sound a note of caution here. It would be naïve to think that there are many professionals who are out there waiting for some great idea to come along and then they are going to religiously reflect on their practice each and every week. It would be a very unusual and dedicated person who could sustain such an approach for any length of time.

It is clear that, whilst reflection is valuable and beneficial, it is something that is not going to always top the list of priorities in any profession. It needs to be worked at and it needs a high level of commitment even to make the time to give it a chance. This book aims to target students and emerging professionals (as well as the seasoned professionals who are interested enough to read it and come on board too) because it is believed that starting such professional reflections early on in your career provides the best chance of it becoming integrated into daily practice. The hope then is that starting off with a culture of reflection, with a clear understanding, structure and set of skills, it may be possible to begin to change the culture. If more professionals saw the process as easy, useful, manageable and professionally supportive, then the word might spread. More and more people would be willing to: Stop; Think; Reflect; Construct understanding; Plan and Act. 'Reflection has to be purposeful, rigorous and take on a critical dimension in order to bring about change. The process of reflection rests on asking probing questions' (Forde and O'Brien, 2011: 29).

Who is it All For?

If you are an individual student or professional who wants to make reflection an integral part of your practice, you would be advised to find a like-minded colleague first to support and encourage you. If you are fortunate enough to do so, you will both reap the benefits. Without such a colleague who knows and understands what you 'are up to', it will be difficult to find someone to support you with your reflections.

If you are in a situation where there is a group of people interested, then there is much more to be gained from the collective experience and the variety of voices doing the reflecting. Students and teachers, in the situation where reflection is being approached as a whole-staff initiative, have perhaps the best chance of success. Certainly if someone else is making the arrangements, providing the training, supporting the implementation of the interactions, as well as supporting the development needs identified, then you are very fortunate.

Larger establishments and institutions have a great opportunity to introduce a culture of supportive interactions. Whilst the ethos advocated in this book is about the reflection not being imposed, and about individual autonomy to create the agenda and be involved in authentic professional personal reflection, it would be true to say that most of us need a little 'push' to get started. As an institution, you might be in a position to say to your staff, yes there is scope for autonomy and for the reflection to be personal, but you 'must' nevertheless 'do it' and be able to demonstrate, by one means or another, that you are doing it.

And yet this is an aspect that many of us shy away from. It is this criticality which challenges our taken-for-granted techniques, attitudes and values. Bolton (2010: 12) suggests that:

> Values in practice are rarely analysed or questioned. Espoused values are recognized and routinely stated both by organizations and individuals. Through reflexive practice professionals realize dissonance between their own values in practice and their espoused values, or those of their organization, leading them to make dynamic change.

A Management Role?

The more people that are involved in such voluntary practice, the more likely it is that positive change might occur, yet this does need courage and commitment. For students and emerging professionals, there is a survival instinct to keep your head below the parapet. This might be wise, but is it providing the space needed for self-discovery and personal professional development? Might some focus on reflection and an ethos of analysing practice provide a more vibrant workforce? In an age of accountability and over-management, it is essential that staff feel some degree of control over their professional lives. It is important that we strive to develop for ourselves, as well as for management. It is essential that any concept of reflection contains these important aspects of self-development rather than becoming just another management tool.

Yet the irony is that it may take action from that very management to make sure that staff and students do try it. This is not like your mother telling you to try the sprouts because they are good for you, but more like her telling you that the strange-looking dish offered to you is worth trying, because once tasted you will be happy to return for more!

Realistically, it will take some support to encourage students and staff to reflect on a regular basis. Time will be the main argument against it happening and this book has tried to show that this should not really be an issue, with a half hour per week the maximum required.

Probably the most telling response we received in researching this book can be found in the answer below:

Question: *If you think peer learning interactions are so interesting and useful why do you not do them on a regular basis?*

Answer: *Well yes, they are good, and it is important to reflect like this, but nobody makes you do it, so you never quite get around to it.* (Bob, primary school teacher)

This is the challenge, but a challenge that those in authority can help us with without detracting from the important elements of personalization and the non-judgmental strengths of the approach.

It is hoped that through the reading of this book, and through trying some of the activities suggested, you may already be well on your way to developing a more habitual approach towards reflection. If so, then regardless of the kind of reflection you are obliged to be part of, the ideas in this book should have prepared you to consider your practice in a safe and structured way, to practise articulating your developing understanding, and to present ideas and plans to improve your practice in an effective and articulate manner. Thereafter, whether it is the dreaded tutor visit, the Ofsted inspector, the learning rounds or a visit from the parents' committee, you will be much more confident to discuss what you do, how you do it, why you do it, and most importantly what it is that is good about it.

The importance of reflection is evident from all of the rhetoric evident anywhere you look, such as in policy statements like the following:

> A new 'Standard for Active Registration' should be developed to clarify expectations of how fully registered teachers are expected to continue to develop their skills and competences. This standard should be challenging and aspirational, fully embracing enhanced professionalism for teachers in Scotland. (Scottish Government, 2011)

The OECD report 'Teachers Matter' studied approaches to teacher quality in 25 countries and concluded that 'there are major concerns about the limited connections between teacher education, teachers' professional development, and school needs'. We need to ensure an appropriate balance and synthesis between individual teacher CPD and school and system level improvement. The majority of teachers in a study by Hustler et al. (2003: 57) reported that school development needs took precedence over their individual learning needs. Larger generic staff development events need to be blended with individual, tailored support to maximise the impact of CPD (Donaldson, 2010: 69).

A three-year evaluation of the Early Professional Development (EPD) Pilot Scheme in England (Moor et al., 2005: 34) reported that mentoring at an early career stage had a positive impact on mentees' teaching practice, career development and commitment to the teaching profession. The EPD evaluation reported 'strong evidence that the early professional development of teachers had led to them becoming more effective members of their school communities' (Donaldson, 2010: 69).

It is clear that in other professions, like the medical profession and in social work, professional reflection is very much valued and on the political agenda. It may be that some of the ideas in this book will support those involved to introduce and develop approaches that meet some of the challenges to reflection cited above.

This book has had as its focus the professional reflection of teachers and student teachers. However, most of the ideas and approaches discussed in the book could apply equally to other professionals and other contexts, the basic premise being that we learn from reflection about how we learn. If we know how we learn well, then we will learn well.

Variations

Of course, we cannot expect professionals to keep on doing the same thing in the same way all of the time, even when they are reflecting. It is important to try to keep things fresh, authentic and useful. Below are some ideas for varying the way that interactions are conducted:

- general
- follow-up
- focused
- artefacts from practice
- experiments on practice.

General

We have already explored in this book the nature of the general reflection which might be the product of our daily practice. This kind of reflection might be a good starting place, but sometimes it will be necessary to depart from the normal process.

Follow-up

It might be that there needs to be some reflection which has its focus on a development that was discussed in an earlier interaction. During some interactions, there might be a decision or an action plan that needs to be implemented. Having some kind of follow-up discussion in the reflective interaction would enable this to be considered in much more professional detail.

Focused

Similarly, there may be times when the person planning to do the reflection will nominate something that they want to focus on. Whether the partner will be observing or not, it is sometimes beneficial to be able to decide in advance on an area of practice that, for whatever reason, they wish to focus on. Indeed, this might in fact link in to the 'lesson study' approach mentioned earlier in this book.

Artefacts

It might be useful sometimes for the person reflecting to bring with them some artefact or evidence of their practice as a focus for discussion. For example, in teaching it may be a piece of artwork, a story or piece of work from a pupil or a worksheet or resource created for a specific lesson. Having this at the meeting might enable a closer look at practice in terms of the materials used or the product of the learning. Not only does this benefit the interaction, it can in some cases help the person reflecting to explore areas of practice that they might not otherwise do in any detail.

Experiments

It might also be the case that part of reflection is to be a problem-solving experience where reflection leads to an analysis of a problem.

The consequence of this might be a plan to try out in practice. This will no doubt lead to some follow-up reflections another time.

There are many possibilities for varying when, how and with whom we reflect, just as long as we strive to meet up and reflect on a regular basis.

Reflecting on Reflections

Reflecting on reflections, I realize that in writing this book I have been able to crystallize what, for me, is important about reflection and the kind of things that get in the way of doing it on a regular basis. The ideas suggested are an attempt to bring together the different theories and approaches, and present strategies to meet these challenges. The aim is to encourage a way forward so that, with support, we can develop our practice through having opportunity to: stop, think, articulate, plan and practice.

Having looked at a range of approaches towards professional reflections, it would be nice and simple to say, yes, this is the one foolproof pedagogy that will suit all learners in all contexts – but of course it is not as simple as that at all.

We have looked at a spectrum of approaches from the controlling and judgemental to the facilitative and personal. All have something positive to offer. The different concept of reflective practice might be seen as some kind of continuum from personal 'discovery' or a counselling model at one extreme to a directive institutional instructing at the other.

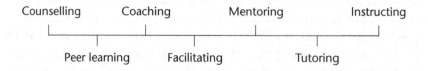

PGDE students who explored this process commented thus:

We were very conscious of not prompting when we were doing it.

The person asking the questions asked the questions and then sat back. They tried not to prompt at all. And then after allowing the person to fully reflect,

then we had a bit more of a general chat and talked about practice and different things we could do to improve. It was more of a conversation after, because
we wanted to share our ideas.

I think the interaction should have different phases, counselling/facilitating
role, as you are listening, then you might have a joint constructing role –
developing understanding, and then you can be together planning what to do
next. I guess one person might take on more of a mentoring role, for example
if they have done this kind of lesson before or if they have more expertise, this
would be the time to share it.

We didn't just use it as reflection, we also used it as a support for each other
too. (Sue and Kelly, PGDE students)

This notion of a varied approach based on personal need and professional development is echoed by Forde and O' Brien (2011: 31):
'There is not one particular pedagogy that holds the key to professional learning, but instead, the optimum is to draw from a range
of pedagogies in the design and delivery of professional learning
opportunities.'

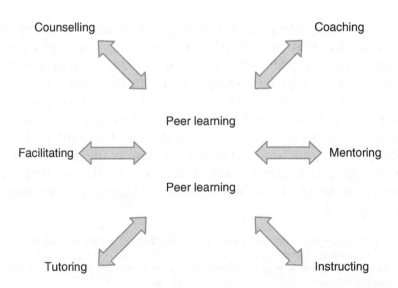

There can be a symbiotic relationship between the Peer Learning Interactions
and the other pedagogies for reflection. Each can be supportive of the other.

Figure 9.1

If we consider that each of these pedagogies has something positive to offer, then we should look at professional reflection as something which can draw on all of these approaches:

- **Counselling, Peer Learning and Coaching** – this is about self-discovery, self-knowledge and behavioural change.

- **Facilitating/Mentoring** – this is about someone more knowledgeable supporting, scaffolding and teaching another to develop their practice.

- **Tutoring/Instructing** – this is about a more didactic approach where someone more knowledgeable explains, scaffolds, builds knowledge and understanding in order that you might develop your practice.

Indeed, in this book we have considered how we might draw upon these in a raft of measures (Chapter 5) or even to employ a range of them within one interaction.

Combining Roles

Beyond the raft of experiences mentioned earlier in the book, there is the notion that even during an interaction we might need to adapt and develop the roles we have to play. We might begin by listening and adopt a **counselling/facilitating** role, as the other person articulates their reflections, and then moving on through the interaction, work more as **coach** or **mentor**, scaffolding and guiding them to more discovery. Later still, there might be a **co-collaborator, joint researcher** role to play, as the quest for greater knowledge and understanding develops, and this in turn might involve reference to another authority or expert who can **teach** us new approaches.

> The crucial aspect is not just a process of reflection on experience but the seeking and using of a range of sources of knowledge including theoretical and research based knowledge in order to ground learning and practice in a sound theoretical frame. (Forde and O'Brien, 2011: 30)

This is where the notion of teachers as action researchers comes in. Having discussed practice and found that something works well, or something that isn't working, the next step is to look at the reasons why. This might involve another look at what we do, or it might involve looking elsewhere for information. Finding this theoretical or research-based evidence provides us with support, justification and above all 'illumination'. It helps us to better understand the relationship between our practice and the theories that explain it. This information in turn enables us to better articulate what we are doing. It enhances our vocabulary and our ability to examine critically what we are doing. This criticality is not just about unpicking something that went badly. It is about understanding what is happening and why. 'For professional learning for teachers to be successful three overarching and essential components are often identified: reflection, dialogue and criticality' (Burley and Pomphrey, 2011: 22).

In this book, we have looked in detail at reflection and its link to professionalism. We have employed dialogue as a phase in the articulation of these reflections and we have invoked criticality as a tool for unlocking these reflections. We have moved beyond these, beyond the mirror's surface and suggested ways of looking back in a manner that influences how we look forward. As Biggs points out, 'a reflection in a mirror is an exact replica of what is in front of it. Reflection in professional practice, however, gives back not what it is, but what *might* be, an improvement on the original' (1999: 6).

It is hoped that this book will enable the reader to review what is meant by reflective practice, and that they will understand why and how it is done. They will see a number of ideas and suggestions about creating a structure for their professional reflection – either as individuals or as part of a bigger organization. They will also see an opportunity to develop their skills and understanding of reflection through the experience of introducing it to others, either through the ideas in Chapter 4 for adults, or in Chapter 7 for children.

The book ends with a series of useful pages to help you to get started on this journey, with a reflective question bank, some pro formas for structuring reflections and some ideas for working with children.

So, not a mirror at all, not a reflection.

Instead, the mirror takes the enlightenment from looking analytically at the past and then projects it forward. This projection, however, may need to distort it, to evaluate and possibly change, adapt, develop, so that the future builds upon and betters the past.

Thus, it is not just a reflection, but something much, much more.

Summary

In this chapter, we considered some of the benefits of reflection. We considered peer learning interactions and some of the challenges that come with them. The important role of managers was explored and their responsibility to play a leading role in enabling such reflections to take place on a regular basis. We also considered ways of making the approach adaptable so that it does not become stale and repetitive. A sense of an interaction where roles are changing and developing was explored. Finally, the idea of reflection being 'more than a simple mirror' was stated.

Questions for Reflection

- Make a list of the variety of roles that might be part of facilitating a peer learning interaction. Think about the kind of skills and questions you might need to employ them.
- Look at the question bank and the pro formas – do they provide sufficient support for these different roles?
- Can you think of additional questions or alternative ways of structuring an interaction so that you feel confident to take on and use the different pedagogies?
- Make a list of artefacts associated with your profession that might enable a focus on practice. Consider the strengths and challenges of having such an approach.
- Make an action plan now to try out some of the ideas in this book.
- Try to experience the empowerment and the benefits of sharing reflections in a non-judgemental environment.
- Try not to let TIME become an insurmountable obstacle!

Further Reading

- Bolton G. (2010) 'Through the mirror', chapter 4. *Reflective Practice*, 3rd edn. London: Sage.
- Bolton G. (2010) 'Reflective practice: other methods', chapter 11. *Reflective Practice,* 3rd edn. London: Sage.
- Brookfield, (1995) 'Negotiating risk,' chapter 11. *Becoming a Critically Reflective Teacher.* San Francisco: Jossey-Bass.
- Brookfield, (1995) 'Creating a culture,' chapter 12. *Becoming a Critically Reflective Teacher.* San Francisco: Jossey-Bass.
- Brookfield, (1995) 'Surprised by the familiar: what autobiographies reveal', chapter 4. *Becoming a Critically Reflective Teacher.* San Francisco: Jossey-Bass.

- Ghaye, A. and Ghaye, K. (1998) 'Reflection on improvement: the validation of practice', chapter 5. *Teaching and Learning Through Critical Reflective Practice*. London: David Fulton Publishers.

References

Biggs, J. (1999) *Teaching for Quality Learning at University*. Buckingham: Open University Press.

Bolton, G. (2010) *Reflective Practice*, 3rd edn. London: Sage.

Burley and Pomphrey (2011) p22–25 cited in Forde, C. and O'Brien, J.

Donaldson, E. (2010) *Teaching Scotland's Future: Report of a Review of Scottish Government Teacher Education in Scotland* – The Report Setting out the Findings of the Review of Teacher Education. Edinburgh: Scottish Government. Available at http: www.Scotland.gov.uk.resource/doc/337626/0110852.pdf

Fanghanel, J. (2004) 'Capturing dissonance in university teacher education environments,' *Studies in Higher Education*, 29(5), 575–90.

Forde, C. and O'Brien, J. (2011) 'Policy and practice in education', no.29. *Coaching and Mentoring: Developing Teachers and Leaders*. Edinburgh: Dunedin Academic Press.

Ghaye, A. and Ghaye, K. (1998) *Teaching and Learning through Critical Reflective Practice*. London: David Fulton.

OECD (2005) *Teachers Matter: Attracting, Developing and Returning Effective Teachers. Directorate for Education*. Available at: http.//www.oecd.org.document/52/0,3746, en_2649_392_63231_3499 1988_1_1_1_1,oohtml.

Appendices

The following are some useful resources and ideas for introducing reflective practice in your setting. They are all photocopiable for your use in the classroom.

Appendix 1: Peer Learning Interactions: Question Bank

Introductory questions	• Talk me through what happened. • Were there any surprises? • What pleased you most? • What was disappointing?
Context Content	• What was the purpose of the lesson? • What did the children learn today that they did not already know? • What did you want the children to remember from this lesson? • What do you think they will remember?
Evaluation Evidence	• Do you think the class learned what you wanted them to? • How do you know?
Prediction Next steps	• What will you do to support and develop this next time? • How will you provide support for all learners? • How will you know if this is successful?
Analysis	• What kind of thinking did you encourage today? • How do you know? • How might a similar lesson be presented differently? • Can you say the extent to which 'thinking about children as learners' influenced the approach that you adopted? • How did your lesson encourage the development of their conceptual understanding? • Can you tell me some links between your lesson and your professional reading? • Tell me about the impact of your lesson on the child's learning. • How has your input enriched the children's progress?
Research	• Can you describe another lesson where content and purpose influenced you to use a different approach?
Summary	• What kind of feedback would you give yourself for this lesson?

 Reflective Practice and Professional Development © Peter Tarrant, 2013

Appendix 2: Reflective Practice Record Pro Forma 1

Reflections of:
Date:
Focus of discussion:
Planned next steps:
What success will look like:
Evidence of success:
Next meeting planned for:

 Reflective Practice and Professional Development © Peter Tarrant, 2013

Appendix 3: Reflective Practice Record Pro Forma 2

FOCUS	COMMENT
Details of the context used for this reflection	
Why was this context chosen for reflection?	
What did you want the pupils to learn?	
What do you think they will remember?	
What kind of thinking did you wish to promote?	
How did you organize the lesson to be inclusive for all learners?	
Were there any particular challenges or issues during the lesson?	

Was there something you were particularly pleased with?	
Was there any sense of frustration during the course of the lesson?	
How might you do things differently another time?	
How will you assess the impact of these changes?	
What might your evidence be?	
What will success/progress look like?	
What did you learn about yourself/ your practice from this reflection?	
Action/plan for next steps	

Appendix 4: Meta-learning Workshop

Reflection and self-evaluation are terms commonly used in relation to teachers and their professional development.

Pupils are also encouraged to reflect upon what and how they learn. This reflection is manifested in the form of learning journeys, learning journals, personal learning plans, etc.

The objective is to look at how we equip pupils to articulate their thinking and how we enable them to think and talk about their learning in a useful and meaningful way.

It is important that we do more than enable pupils to 'fill in the boxes' about reflection. They need to be able to reflect and see which kinds of learning they are good at, and to realize why this is. They need to see where they need to work harder, or *differently*, and to have some strategies to employ to achieve personal progress.

To sum up, pupils need to be able to complete the following four statements:

1 I learn best when........

2 The kind of learning and thinking I am doing is.........

3 When learning is difficult I can.........

4 I know I've learnt well when............

Making formerly unconscious, intangible,
or reflexive processes or events, explicit.

Activity for Staff (Working in Groups of Three)

Look first at the yellow cards:

Think of an area of the curriculum, and a lesson, that one of you has taught recently that was, for some reason, memorable. In a couple of sentences, write down what it was that you wanted the children to learn.

Look now at the blue learning cards:

Discuss which of these *kinds of learning* the pupils were engaged in. Choose up to four blue learning cards.

Look now at the green learning cards:

Discuss which *learning skills* the pupils were engaged in. Choose up to four green learning cards.

Think back to your lesson aims:

Ask yourself:

Did I share with the children *what* they learnt?

Did I share with the children *how* they learnt?

Am I teaching in a way that encourages this kind of learning?

Am I making it clear to pupils that they are developing these kinds of learning and these learning skills?

Would they benefit as learners, if they had a better idea that these learning skills were part of the learning intentions?

If you did this activity with a group of pupils, what kind of questions might you ask when you looked at the cards they had selected?

Meta-cognition:

Meta-cognition can be broken down into different categories: task awareness, strategy awareness, skills awareness, performance awareness, reflective awareness and emotive awareness.

Meta-cognitive thinking

Task awareness	Did you know what to do?
What to do Why How to begin the task How this learning links to other learning Checking and improving	What did you do? What did you learn? Why was this important?

Strategy awareness	Did you know how to do it?
Organizing Adapting Persevering Concentrating Investigating Creating/imagining Experimenting Guessing Predicting	How did you go about the task? What kind of thinking did you use on this task? Did you have a good plan?
Skills awareness	**Did you know which skills you used?**
Remembering Understanding Checking Problem solving Presenting Making connections	What skills did you need? What strategies did you need to use?
Performance awareness	**Did you know how well you did it?**
Contributing Sharing Supporting Cooperating Taking advice	How well did you work with others? Did you support anyone else's learning? Did you use any ideas or advice from them?
Reflective awareness	**Did you know how you learned?**
Looking back and reflecting Realizing what was good Seeing ways to improve Evaluating strategies Planning next steps	What were you pleased with? What did you find hard? What seemed easy? What might you have done differently? What might you do next time?
Emotive awareness	**Did you know how your learning 'felt?'**
Considering how the learning 'felt' Making links between feeling and learning	What did you like/dislike? How did you feel when…? How would you feel if…?

Task for Volunteers

- Choose at least two lessons to focus on over the next two weeks.

- Look at your learning intentions and see if there are opportunities to make the learning to learn more explicit.

- You might use the list and questions as a focus, or you might use the card activity, or you might have ideas of your own.

- Try flagging the learning at the beginning and end of the lesson.

- Keep a note of the elements that you choose as your focus.

- Keep a note of some of the pupil responses.

- You might, for example, highlight some of the things on the questions sheet to monitor the kind of things you manage to profile.

Example

Lesson on floating and sinking.

Outline Learning Intentions and Success Criteria.

Also discuss some of the learning skills such as: organizing, experimenting, checking, cooperating.

As the lesson progresses, remind them of the kind of thinking and learning that they are involved in – use the vocabulary when you can, put it on display or on a Smartboard for them to see.

At the end of the session, go over what they have learned, but also go over how they learned, drawing attention to key skills with questions such as:

How did you decide how to organize the materials?

Was this a good way, or not?

How did you check your work? Were there other ways?

Do you feel that you were well organized? Did your approach to this task work?

How might you do it better another time?

What advice would you give to someone like you doing this activity for the first time?

Did you learn anything about your own learning approaches today?

It is not necessary to add anything extra for this, instead the idea is that you look for opportunities to make learning how we learn more explicit. You are introducing the tools and the vocabulary for pupils to be more meta-aware.

Keep a note of the kind of things you choose as your focus and the kind of responses you get.

Reflective Practice and Professional Development © Peter Tarrant, 2013

Appendix 5: Vocabulary Cards

Yellow cards

reading	writing	maths	project	art
drama	gym	music	group work	health

Blue cards

wondering	exploring	thinking	testing	trying out
guessing	choosing	deciding	suggesting	estimating

Green cards

trying	thinking	concentrating	taking care	using my plan
working out	problem-solving	trying different ways	making connections	remembering other learning

Group skill cards

cooperating	being a good team member	sharing	considering others	supporting others	

Review/reflection skill cards

remembering	checking	considering	noticing	improving	
redrafting	showing others	adding more detail	making changes	making connections	

Emotional responses to learning cards

confident	anxious	excited	bored	enthusiastic
happy	frustrated	confused	relaxed	curious

Reflective Practice and Professional Development © Peter Tarrant, 2013

Appendix 6: Interviewing for Learning

The following criteria were devised by a Primary Seven class in Scotland.

The advice is just as pertinent to adults conducting peer learning interactions.

Advice for a good interview:

Give eye contact

Look interested

Start with closed questions

Work up to open questions

Listen well and build connecting questions

React positively

Smile and encourage

Some challenges:

Trying not to laugh

Thinking what to ask

Being able to think of 'piggy-back' questions

Having too many questions in your head

Feeling embarrassed and 'rubbish at this'

Appendix 7: Focus for Learning

Content

Today I am going to ask you to think about...... (tick which one)

---

a recent lesson ☐

the lesson your teacher has suggested that you talk about ☐

the learning approach or skill suggested by your teacher ☐

Can you tell me a little bit about this?

What kind of learning was this?

What did you find easy about doing this?

What was challenging?

What helped you?

What got in the way of your learning?

Can you tell me how you ....?

Was there one thing you can take from this lesson and use again and again in other situations?

What advice would you give to someone else doing this lesson/skill?

How did your teacher help your learning?

In what way did you help someone else or did they help you?

Is there anything else about learning that you can tell me?

Reflective Practice and Professional Development © Peter Tarrant, 2013

Appendix 8: Meta-learning for Pupils

Thinking about thinking and learning

Think of a lesson you have done this week that is memorable for some reason.

Below are some words to describe the kind of learning and thinking you might have been doing.

Look at each group of words and highlight one or two that best describe the learning that you were doing.

The lesson I am thinking of was:

In the lesson we were to:

At the beginning of the task the learning and thinking I was doing was:

wondering	exploring	investigating	testing	hypothesizing
guessing	predicting	thinking	suggesting	estimating
imagining	creating	choosing	deciding	planning
rehearsing	practising	modelling	sketching out	

During the task, the learning and thinking I was doing was:

trying	persevering	concentrating	taking care	using my plan
working out	problem solving	trying different ways	making connections	remembering other learning
using advice	recording	researching	looking up	checking information
cooperating	being a good team member	sharing	considering others	supporting others

At the end of the task, the learning and thinking I was doing was:

remembering	reviewing	checking		
considering	noticing	evaluating		
redrafting	improving	adding more detail	making changes	
listening	telling	asking	repeating	explaining
summarizing	making connections	demonstrating	presenting	

My feelings during this learning were:

confident	anxious	excited	bored	enthusiastic
happy	satisfied	amazed	relaxed	curious
hurt	fed up	irritated	embarrassed	frustrated
confused	scared	fascinated	angry	delighted

Next time I would like to improve my learning and thinking by:

Appendix 9: Questions on What and How we Learn

Tell me something you remember from the lesson.

Was there something you liked you could tell me about?

Was there something you didn't like that you could tell me about?

Tell me about something you thought was a bit difficult.

Tell me if there was something you found too easy.

What do you think you learned about the lesson?

Did you learn anything about your own learning?

What helped you to learn?

Did anything get in the way of your learning?

Do you think you had to work hard in what you did or in your thinking?

Tell me about this – why was it hard or easy for you?

Have you done anything like this before?

If so, can you tell me what was similar and what was different?

What could you do to make your learning about this kind of thing better?

How would you describe your feelings when you were asked to do the activities?

Do you have any advice to give yourself, your friends or your teacher about this lesson?

Tell me about.......?

What was it that ....?

Have you ever ....?

Do you always ....?

Couldn't you have ....?

Why didn't you ....?

Would you ....?

What did you ....?

Can you remember ....?

Reflective Practice and Professional Development © Peter Tarrant, 2013

Index

Reference Index